"STOP HER!" NANCY SHOUTED, "DON'T LET HER GET
AWAY!"

The Secret at Shadow Ranch. Page 181

"WHAT ARE YOU DOING HERE?" HE DEMANDED HARSHLY.
The Secret at Shadow Ranch.

Page 118

TAKING AIM, NANCY FIRED AT THE LYNX.

The Secret at Shadow Ranch.

Page 80

NANCY CLUTCHED THE BRIDLE OF BESS' PONY.

The Secret at Shadow Ranch. *Frontispiece (Page 44)*

NANCY DREW MYSTERY STORIES

THE SECRET AT SHADOW RANCH

BY

CAROLYN KEENE

Author of "The Secret of the Old Clock,"
"The Hidden Staircase," Etc.

ILLUSTRATED BY
RUSSELL H. TANDY

WITH AN INTRODUCTION BY
MILDRED WIRT BENSON

FACSIMILE EDITION

BEDFORD, MASSACHUSETTS
APPLEWOOD BOOKS

For further information about these editions, please write:
Applewood Books, Box 365, Bedford, MA 01730.

LIBRARY OF CONGRESS CATALOGING-IN-PUBLICATION DATA
Keene, Carolyn.
    The secret at shadow ranch / by Carolyn Keene;
illustrated by Russell H. Tandy; with an introduction by
Mildred Wirt Benson.—Facsimile ed.
        p.   cm.   —(Nancy Drew mystery stories)
    Summary: While staying at a ranch in Arizona,
Nancy Drew becomes involved in a mystery surrounding
a mistreated child.
ISBN: 1-55709-159-5
    [1. Mystery and detective stories.]   I. Tandy,
Russell H., ill.   II. Title.   III. Series: Keene, Carolyn.
Nancy Drew mystery stories.
PZ7.K23Sb   1994
[Fic]—dc20   94-9296
                                         CIP
                                          AC

10 9 8 7 6 5

PUBLISHER'S NOTE

Much has changed in America since the Nancy Drew series first began in 1930. The modern reader may be delighted with the warmth and exactness of the language, the wholesome innocence of the characters, their engagement with the natural world, or the nonstop action without the use of violence; but just as well, the modern reader may be extremely uncomfortable with the racial and social stereotyping, the roles women play in these books, or the use of phrases or situations which may conjure up some response in the modern reader that was not felt by the reader of the times.

For good or bad, we Americans have changed quite a bit since these books were first issued. Many readers will remember these editions with great affection and will be delighted with their return; others will wonder why we just don't let them disappear. These books are part of our heritage. They are a window on our real past. For that reason, except for the addition of this note and the introduction by Mildred Wirt Benson, we are presenting *The Secret at Shadow Ranch* unedited and unchanged from its first edition.

MORE ABOUT NANCY

By
MILDRED WIRT BENSON
AUTHOR OF
PENNY PARKER MYSTERY STORIES;
DANGEROUS DEADLINE;
TWIN RING MYSTERY; QUARRY GHOST,
& OTHERS

NANCY DREW, the super solver of mysteries, has yet to come up with an explanation in the hitherto unknown Case of the Missing Ledger.

Strange indeed, that a puzzle without solution—one which involved her own existence as a fictional character, concerned the odd disappearance and amazing recovery of an author's battered old record book with entries in faded but legible ink.

The ledger's first notation was in 1921, recording a 16-year-old's first sale of a short story, "Midget," to the Nazarene Publishing Co. for $3.50.

In 1929, when *Secret of the Old Clock*, the initial volume in the Nancy Drew series, was accepted for publication by the Stratemeyer Syndicate and Grosset and Dunlap, New York, the event was duly recorded.

Thereafter, for 30 years, until *Quarry Ghost* (Dodd, Mead) marked the end of the author's fictional writing, each of nearly 100 short stories and more than 130 published books faithfully were listed.

The old ledger took on more significance as the years rolled by. With its owner, it moved from Iowa to Cleveland, and then to Toledo, Ohio. Usually it was stored in a desk or a filing cabinet.

After 1959, no new entries were made, and suddenly the old record book disappeared. At times, it was sorely needed to verify a sale date or other information, but repeated searches never brought it to light.

Nancy herself took no interest in the mystery, and in time the old account book was all but forgotten.

Then one day, a decision was made to paint the basement floor and recreation room of my home. In the process, a heavy, old metal filing cabinet had to be moved.

There beneath it, plastered to the cement floor, was the long-lost ledger!

How did it get into such a strange place? No one had the slightest idea. If Nancy knew the answer, she was disinclined to share her secret.

Miraculously, the old book had withstood years of dampness, remaining legible and in good condition. Clearly, it pinpointed 1929 as the date when the first Nancy Drew story was written and sold by me to the Stratemeyer Syndicate, then of New York City.

The Secret at Shadow Ranch, one of my favorite stories because of its western setting, lists in the old ledger as the fifth volume in the series. Written and published in 1930, it followed three Ruth Fieldings assigned to me by the syndicate and another three girls' aviation books under my own name for the Barse Publishing Co.

By then, I was teaching swimming but also writing steadily, usually with complete concentration. Often, while my husband worked a night shift for the Associated Press at a Cleveland newspaper, I would set my typewriter on an upended orange crate in the tiny kitchen of our rented apartment, and hammer away.

One evening, while writing one of the early Nancy Drews, I followed my usual practice of simultaneously preparing a meal. The caramelized dessert I was trying for the first time entailed the boiling of an unopened can of condensed milk.

So engrossed did I become in Nancy's adventures that I lost all count of time. Ears were dead to the hissing of steam from the nearby stove as the pan of water ran dry.

Suddenly, in series book style, there was a mighty blast!

The sealed can of milk shot like a missile to the ceiling. Exploding, it splattered a huge blob of dark brown goo on the white wallpaper above my head. As a result of this mishap, we moved to a new, better apartment.

As I recall, *Shadow Ranch* was a breeze to write, a fun experience. Unfamiliar subject matter never daunted me. I merely waded in, gathering material as I wrote. I had made vacation trips to Colorado and the West, but never to a ranch. The Cleveland public library was a great source of information, and as usual, my imagination filled in any blanks.

From the first chapter, the story moved smoothly. Horseback riding was not one of my sports, but I had taken a few jaunts through a Cleveland park area, on one occasion crossing a shallow river. Unaccustomed to an inept rider, the horse balked in midstream.

The incident was insignificant. However, when Nancy and her friends later made an exploratory ride into the mountains, my imagination enlarged it into an exciting scene. The sluggish stream became a roaring torrent, horses took on racetrack spirit, and as usual, Nancy effortlessly rescued the ever-timid Bess Marvin.

A subsequent ride into wilderness brought on the inevitable storm, usually included in each syndicate plot. This one was entirely to my liking, leading logically to Nancy's meeting with a mysterious old woman who lived in a dilapidated shack in the woods. In my style of writing, nearly all shacks were run down and villains could usually be identified by their crude manners or penetrating eyes.

In *Shadow Ranch*, as the three friends become better riders, they venture deeper into the wilds. After being stalked by a cougar, Nancy, on advice of her elders, carries a revolver for protection and uses it when an emergency arises.

A few critics have voiced disapproval of any mention of firearms in children's literature. Scenes, which include the shooting of a lynx, were dictated by syndicate plot, and at the time, long before animal rights or violence became an issue, seemed quite natural.

In *Shadow Ranch*, readers are introduced to the supporting characters of the plump Bess Marvin and the boyish George Fayne. Whatever became of early "chums," I never knew. However, I assumed that syndicate owners selected Nancy's new friends to provide contrast. Also, for a brief time in the early 1900s, it was a fad to give male names to fictional female characters.

As I gained book writing experience, I gradually picked up speed and rhythm. In those days there were no computers or copying machines. A poorly constructed or mistyped sentence meant a lost page. Many times, though unnecessary, I rewrote and rewrote, merely to achieve simplicity or a certain word sound or narrative flow.

Purposely, sentences were made short, designed to keep the story moving. Grammatical construction making use of the introductory participial phrase came naturally to me. This style of writing sometimes has been referred to as "a Nancy Drewism," because of its frequent use in the series. Such phrases were especially helpful to me in making rapid transitions from scene to scene.

For example, in Chapter Two of *Shadow Ranch*, Nancy and her friends are traveling by train en route to the West. A typical "work horse" sentence reads:

"Returning to her own Pullman car, Nancy dismissed the stranger from her thoughts."

In a few words, a scene transition has been achieved, yet emphasis remains upon the mystery.

Use of active verbs was helpful in the writing of narration. Descriptions of more than a sentence or two usually were avoided, but I did grope for words such as "spooky," "creepy," "eerie," and the like, to build up atmosphere. My goal always was to keep readers glued to the pages through emotional impact rather than by recounting one exciting incident after another.

Simple writing is never easy to achieve. However, I discovered early on that the more time I devoted to eliminating complicated or wordy sentences, the easier it was for readers to follow my thoughts.

Some critics have referrred to "invisible style" in the early Nancy Drew stories, commenting that while vocabulary was ample, my writing was lacking in language. The meaning of this never was clear.

Admittedly, I did race through a story, deliberately heightening action by making Nancy emotionally indifferent to it. Whether lost in the woods with her friends, trapped by fire or flood, secreted in a packing box, or imprisoned in a tower or an old house, the invincible girl sleuth always kept her cool.

Through it all, Nancy as I described her retained stability and common sense, delivering an unspoken message of courage and determination. I like to think that these basic qualities and others, which become apparent only after the reading of many volumes in the series, may have distinguished the early tales from those of a later date.

As the treasured old ledger indicated, 1930 was, for me, a most busy writing year. Others followed. Orders came rapidly and at times, I was several manuscripts behind. In addition to syndicate writing, I plotted and developed numerous series and individual mystery stories under my own or chosen pen names. *The Penny Parker Mystery Stories* (Cupples & Leon) especially appealed to me because without editorial direction, I was able to create a Nancy-type character, a bit flip perhaps, but entirely to my liking.

In *Books at Iowa* (1973), I wrote that in my style of series stories, there was no intentional time concept, no specific geographical location, no ties that bound to the past.

"To be remembered for more than an hour, a tale must ride in its own sealed capsule, isolated from everyday living. A presentation should be as true to the aspirations of childhood in the year 2003 as in 1906."

If this sentiment be true, Nancy long will live in memory, untouched by the world about her. Over the years, she may change in appearance and living style, but for early readers or those who discover her for the first time in the Applewood Books, she should forever remain the same — every girl's challenge and dream for a better future.

NANCY DREW MYSTERY STORIES

THE SECRET AT SHADOW RANCH

BY

CAROLYN KEENE

AUTHOR OF "THE SECRET OF THE OLD CLOCK,"
"THE BUNGALOW MYSTERY," ETC.

ILLUSTRATED BY

RUSSELL H. TANDY

NEW YORK
GROSSET & DUNLAP
PUBLISHERS

Made in the United States of America

NANCY DREW
MYSTERY STORIES

By CAROLYN KEENE

12mo. Cloth. Illustrated.

GROSSET & DUNLAP, PUBLISHERS, NEW YORK

CONTENTS

iv Contents

THE SECRET AT SHADOW RANCH

CHAPTER I

AN ENTICING INVITATION

"OH, NANCY, dear, do say you'll go with us to Shadow Ranch!"

"Think of all the fun we can have on a real Western ranch!"

Nancy Drew, curled up like a contented kitten on the living room davenport, smiled at the earnest entreaties of her friends, Elizabeth Marvin and George Fayne. The two girls, both residents of River Heights, had pounced down upon Nancy only a few minutes before and were endeavoring to convince her that nothing could equal a summer vacation spent in the West. With characteristic impetuosity they had demanded a decision before they had furnished the details of the proposed trip.

"It does sound tempting, I'll admit," Nancy said slowly, her blue eyes sparkling with antici-

1

pation. "Shadow Ranch is such an enticing name!"

"And I'm sure it must be an enticing place!" Elizabeth assured her eagerly. "Just think of it—cowboys and bucking broncos and everything."

"I'll leave the cowboys to you since I don't happen to have your flare for the romantic," Nancy laughed. "But tell me what it's all about. So far, all I've gathered is that you want me to go West with you to visit a place called Shadow Ranch."

"You tell her, George."

"Well, it's this way, Nancy. Our uncle, Richard Rawley of Chicago, has come into possession of a small, run-down ranch in Arizona. He had to take it over in payment for a debt."

"That isn't why they call it Shadow Ranch, is it?" Nancy teased.

"Of course not!" George Fayne declared with a toss of her straight brown bob. "I guess they named it that because it's in the shadow of the mountains. Anyway, this ranch is sadly in need of attention as the foreman hasn't been very aggressive. Uncle Dick hasn't the time to go out there and attend to things himself, so he has planned to send Aunt Nell instead."

"You'll like her," Elizabeth broke in.

"She's of a practical turn of mind, but always in for a good time."

"Aunt Nell is to see what can be done with the ranch," George went on. "She simply hates the country and says that if she goes Bess and I must go along to keep her amused."

"But where do I come in?" Nancy demanded.

"I'm coming to that as fast as words will take me. Aunt Nell says we may invite you and one other girl to go along. That will make a jolly foursome."

"How long will you be out there?"

"Well, that all depends on how long it takes to settle Uncle Dick's affairs. Several weeks at least."

"Alice Regor has already promised she'll go," Elizabeth declared.

"Alice Regor?"

"Oh, you've never met her, Nancy. She's Uncle Dick's niece from Baltimore. We're both Aunt Nell's nieces, you know."

"Alice is as pretty as a picture," George supplied. "Not homely like me."

"Why, you're not a bit homely," Nancy assured her promptly. "I think you're quite distinctive looking myself."

"You base flatterer! Look at this straight hair and my pug nose! And everyone says I'm irresponsible and terribly boyish."

"Well, you sort of pride yourself on being

boyish, don't you? Your personality fits in with your name, you will admit."

"I do like my name," George admitted, "but I get tired of explaining to folks that it isn't short for Georgia. Bess doesn't have half the trouble I do."

As she spoke, George glanced up at her cousin as though trying to discover the secret of her dignity and composure. Elizabeth was noted for always doing the correct thing at the correct time. Though she lacked the dash and vivacity of her cousin, she was better looking and dressed with more care and taste. Yet, had a stranger entered the room, he undoubtedly would have looked first at Nancy Drew, for though she could not be termed beautiful, her face was more interesting than that of either of her companions.

"Tell me about this Alice Regor," Nancy commanded with interest.

George and Elizabeth exchanged quick glances. There was a moment of hesitation and then George said:

"I suppose we may as well tell you about it now. You must take care never to ask her about her father."

"Her father?" Nancy gasped. "What has he done? Robbed a bank?"

"Nothing like that. He just disappeared one day."

"That was about eight years ago," Elizabeth explained. "Alice was only seven at the time —she's younger than we are, you know."

"You mean he deserted his wife and child?" Nancy questioned.

"Well, of course that was what everyone said at the time, though his wife never would admit it. She always thought that something dreadful had happened to him. You see, he started off on a business trip to Philadelphia. Apparently he never went there."

"He just quietly disappeared," George added, "and that was the last that was ever heard of him."

"He never wrote to Alice or his wife?"

"Never a word."

"How odd! But I've read about such things happening. Were his business affairs in bad shape?"

"That's what made it all seem so queer," Elizabeth explained. "He had no debts and his business was prosperous."

"Did he have enemies?"

"Not an enemy as far as anyone ever knew," George declared. "It looks as though he just made up his mind to desert his family."

"What a contemptible thing to do!"

"No one could ever understand why he would do such a thing," George continued. "Mrs. Regor is a lovely lady and she was always devoted to her husband. He seemed to think the world of her, too.''

''Naturally, Alice is sensitive about it all,'' Elizabeth said quietly. ''She tries not to let on, but you can tell that she never quite got over the whole affair. She's rather sad sometimes, and though she never says a word, you can tell she's blue about her father.''

''I'll be careful never to mention the subject,'' Nancy promised.

George caught eagerly at her words.

''Then you do intend to go!''

''I didn't say that,'' Nancy protested.

''That's the only way you'll get to meet Alice. You'll like her, I know.''

''I have become interested in her already, George.''

''Then say you'll go. We'll have such a grand summer at Shadow Ranch! What do we care if the place is a little run-down? There will be horses to ride——''

''For those who can ride,'' Elizabeth cut in. ''I never have. You ride, don't you, Nancy?''

''Oh, a little.''

''That probably means you're a regular topnotcher at it. Oh, well, you can teach the rest of us.''

''I should love to go,'' Nancy declared. ''I've never visited an honest-to-goodness ranch. I'll talk to Dad about it and see what he says. I don't like to leave him here alone for such a long time."

"What's that you want to talk to Dad about?" a deep voice demanded.

Of one accord the three girls turned and saw Carson Drew standing in the doorway. Nancy sprang up from the davenport, and, running over to him, caught him eagerly by the arm.

"Oh, Dad, Bess and George want me to go to Arizona for the summer. Their uncle owns a ranch out there."

"Hm," the lawyer considered the matter gravely. "Proper chaperone, eh?"

"Oh, very proper," Bess giggled. "Our Aunt Nell Rawley."

"Anyway, we wouldn't need a chaperone," George declared boldly. "Four girls ought to be able to take care of themselves."

"I wasn't worrying about you. I was thinking about the poor cowboys," Mr. Drew chuckled.

"Oh, Dad, you don't really think I could go, do you?" Nancy began quickly. "I told the girls that if you needed me here——"

"I always need you," her father replied gravely, but with a twinkle in his eye. "However, as it happens, I've been called to the state capital on business and I'm apt to be there for several weeks. Would you rather go there or to Arizona?"

"Arizona!" Nancy replied, but with a guilty look.

Mr. Drew laughed outright.

"That's all right. I'd rather go there myself. I'll manage to get along without you for a few weeks if you'll promise not to get into any mischief."

"I promise."

"And better leave all mysteries alone."

"Oh, Dad, that's not fair!"

"All right, I won't hold you to that promise because I know you're born with the itch in your blood."

"Nancy won't find any mystery at Shadow Ranch," George laughed. "The only queer thing about that place is how it's managed to hold together with such a lazy foreman to look after it."

"I think I'll run up to Canada for a couple of weeks of fishing while you're gone," Mr. Drew told his daughter; "so you see everything will work out very nicely. Of course, I'd like to have you go along, but there will be three men besides the guides, and I couldn't expect the others to enjoy having you as much as I should."

"I rather guess not! I nearly broke up the party the last time I went. It wasn't my fault that I hooked a twelve pound muskie. The poor fish should have known better than to have selected my line.''

''Nancy became a trifle excited,'' Mr. Drew explained gravely.

''Dad is being considerate of my feelings now. The truth of it is that I upset the boat. We lost the fish and the tackle, and I think the others that were with us could have killed me cheerfully.''

''It wasn't that bad, Nancy.''

''Well, anyway, I know I'll not be missed on that fishing trip. Me for Arizona!''

''When do you start?'' Mr. Drew questioned.

Nancy glanced inquiringly at Elizabeth and George.

''Just one week from to-day,'' Elizabeth answered, ''if we can get ready that soon.''

''I can get ready in ten minutes if necessary!'' Nancy cried. ''Oh, what a wonderful summer we're going to have!''

CHAPTER II

OFF FOR SHADOW RANCH

EXCITED at the prospect of spending the summer at Shadow Ranch, Nancy Drew plunged into an orgy of feverish preparation. There were new clothes to buy which necessitated frequent consultations with George Fayne and Bess Marvin who likewise were in a quandary as to what they should take with them. In the end, Nancy wisely purchased only the most simple sport garments and decided upon stout boots and shoes which would resist mountain climbing and all sorts of weather. At the last minute she gave up the idea of a trunk, and by careful planning and packing was able to get everything into two large suitcases and an overnight bag.

"I wonder if I'm taking enough?" she asked her father somewhat doubtfully. "Bess and George will each have a trunk."

"Enough?" Carson Drew demanded with masculine brutality. "When I go to Canada I'll throw everything into one bag!"

At last the appointed day came, and when

Nancy met George and Bess at the railroad station and saw the array of baggage which they were taking, she was thankful that she had pared hers to a minimum. According to the plan, the three girls were to make the trip alone as far as Chicago. There they were to meet Alice Regor and Mrs. Rawley. Carson Drew had accompanied his daughter to the station, and a host of friends had gathered to say goodbye to the girls and to wish them a pleasant vacation. Everyone talked at once and Nancy was showered with candy, books and magazines.

At length the train came puffing into the station and the girls were escorted to their Pullman car.

"Have a good time!" Carson Drew called.

"Don't vamp any of those cowboys!" another shouted as the train began to move slowly out of the station.

The three girls settled themselves comfortably in their section, but they were far too excited to read. Instead, they talked of Shadow Ranch and of the wonderful times which they felt were ahead of them.

As the train carried her rapidly onward, Nancy Drew little dreamed of what really lay before her. She had no thought that she was riding straight into a mystery as baffling as any she had ever solved.

All her life it seemed to Nancy that she had led an exciting existence. Perhaps that was because she was the only daughter of a lawyer who specialized in criminal and mystery cases. Nancy's mother had died only a few years after her birth, and the girl had assumed the management of the Drew household at an early age. She had taken a keen interest in her father's work and frequently had discussed unusual cases with him, but it was quite by accident that she became involved in a baffling mystery of her own.

To the surprise of her father, she had quietly gone about the task of discovering what had become of the Josiah Crowley will, and, as is recounted in the first volume of this series, "The Secret of the Old Clock," had solved the mystery to everyone's satisfaction. After that, it was but a short time until she was engrossed in other cases which had baffled clever detectives.

Her most recent exploit had been the solving of "The Mystery at Lilac Inn." By untangling an almost hopeless maze of evidence, she had caused the arrest of a daring jewel thief and at great personal risk had recovered the inheritance of a friend. Nancy's adventures had brought her considerable publicity; in fact, so great an amount that she had declared she was looking forward with pleasure to a quiet, peaceful summer.

"Aunt Nell has promised to meet us at the Union Station," Bess was saying. "Alice should be there by this time, too. Oh, I hope you'll like her, Nancy."

"I'm sure I shall," Nancy returned. "I'm very much interested in her story."

"You'll not mention a word——"

"Of course not. I'll not let on that I know a thing about her father, and we'll all try to show her as good a time as we can and make her forget her troubles."

The afternoon dragged slowly along, or so it seemed to the three girls who were eager to reach their destination. At last, however, the big train rumbled into the Chicago station.

"Oh, dear," Bess fretted as she looked for a familiar face at the gate. "What if Aunt Nell and Alice shouldn't be here! We have less than an hour to catch our next train. If we miss it our tickets won't be good."

"Do stop worrying," George scolded good-naturedly. "They'll be here all right."

At that moment Nancy caught sight of an attractive lady of perhaps forty years who was waving her hand, and before she could turn to George and Bess the two girls had darted forward to greet her.

"Aunt Nell!" Bess cried. "We were afraid we might miss you in the crowd."

George quickly introduced Nancy to her aunt

and then to Alice Regor who was standing quietly at Mrs. Rawley's side. Alice was indeed as pretty as a picture and when she spoke it was with a soft, drawling voice that captivated Nancy at once. Yet, she could not help noticing that the girl's deep blue eyes were listless and sad save when she smiled.

"Where's Uncle Dick?" George demanded bluntly when the introductions had been completed.

"He'll be here in a minute. He had to see about our tickets. The time of our train has changed and we'll not have many minutes to spare if we're to reach the other station."

At that moment, a pleasant-faced gentleman hurried up to where the party was standing and even before he was presented Nancy knew that he could be none other than Uncle Dick Rawley.

"I'm sorry to rush you off," he apologized; "but if you're to catch your train we'll have to hurry."

A taxi was already waiting at the door, and the girls crowded into it. Before they had exchanged many words they had arrived at their destination and Mr. Rawley was helping them to alight.

"Five minutes left!" he warned them, glancing at his watch.

They rushed madly through the station wait-

ing room, three porters following with hand
luggage. They passed through the gate and
raced toward a long Pullman train. No sooner
had Mr. Rawley settled them in their respective
sections than the porters began to close the
vestibules. Hasty farewells were said, and he
swung to the platform, waving until they were
out of sight.

"Well, we're off!" George remarked.

"And I wonder if I'm still together," Mrs.
Rawley laughed. "That man will be the death
of me one of these days! I wanted to wait for
the next train, but Dick would have it that we
could catch this one."

"And how!" George said slangily. "It
doesn't start out much like a quiet summer."

"I am afraid it will be more quiet than you
girls expect," Mrs. Rawley declared. "As I've
already explained, Shadow Ranch is quite
small." She glanced mischievously at Bess.
"My husband tells me that the cowboys aren't
particularly young or handsome either."

"Poor Bess!" George giggled.

"A lot I care!" Bess announced with a toss
of her head. "I don't see why everyone has
to think I'm romantic!"

"I haven't told you girls the chief draw-
back," Mrs. Rawley continued. "Shadow
Ranch is fifteen miles from the railway station
and a town."

"We'll not mind that," Nancy declared. "I think it will be fun to get out into the wilds."

"So do I," Alice Regor added a trifle wistfully. "I'm so tired of just cities and people."

"Well, I'm afraid I can't share your enthusiasm for the country," Mrs. Rawley said. "I certainly wouldn't have made the trip if it hadn't been necessary. However, with you young things along to entertain me, I'll probably manage to survive."

At first the girls were interested in the country through which they were passing, but as corn and wheat fields began to bore them, they soon brought out the bridge cards..

"I believe I'll go out to the observation car," Nancy remarked. "You'll have a foursome without me, so I won't break up the game."

Leaving the others to enjoy their game, she made her way through the long train and found a chair in the observation car. After a time she picked up a magazine and, noticing an article on Western ranches, read it with considerable interest. Finishing the article, she glanced up and was surprised to see that the man who sat in the chair beside her was regarding her curiously. Caught in the act of staring, he evidently felt that an apology was necessary, for he said politely:

"I beg your pardon, but I couldn't help but

notice that you were reading about our Western ranches.''

Nancy glanced quickly at the man. His hair was streaked with gray and his forehead was deeply lined yet she decided that he could not be more than forty-five years of age. It was his eyes which held her attention, for in expression they were sad, almost tragic.

"Yes, I am interested in Western ranches," she said with a pleasant smile. "You see, I'm planning to spend my summer at Shadow Ranch in Arizona."

"Shadow Ranch!" the man exclaimed. "Well, if that isn't a coincidence."

"You know of the place then?"

"Well, rather. I live at Mougarstown."

Nancy continued to look blank, for the name meant nothing to her.

"That's the nearest town to Shadow Ranch," the man explained. He fumbled in his pocket and brought out a card which he handed Nancy. "I'm Ross Rogers and as you'll see by the card I have a little book and stationery store in Mougarstown."

"Probably you can tell me all about Arizona and Shadow Ranch," Nancy suggested.

Ross Rogers shook his head.

"I've never visited Shadow Ranch, though I've been told it was a profitable place before it was allowed to run down."

Nancy asked a few more questions which the man answered politely, but as he did not seem especially disposed to talk, she soon fell silent. Yet, she could not help but steal an occasional glance at him, and was surprised at the thoughtful, sad expression which had settled upon his face.

"He must have had a great deal of trouble in his life," she told herself.

Nancy was naturally interested in people, yet she was never prying. She felt attracted to Ross Rogers and wondered what the story of his life was, but she had no intention of trying to draw him out.

After a time she arose and left the observation car. Glancing back over her shoulder, she saw that the man was still staring out the window and was evidently not aware that she had departed.

Returning to her own Pullman car, Nancy dismissed the stranger from her thoughts. However, the next morning she entered the dining car with the other girls and to her surprise was seated at a table with Ross Rogers. His pleasure at seeing her again was so genuine that she could not do otherwise than introduce him to the others.

While they waited for breakfast to be served the man chatted pleasantly on impersonal subjects, but Nancy could not help but observe that when the conversation switched to himself, he quickly fell silent.

"That man interests me," she told the girls after they had returned to their own car.

"I don't see anything interesting about him," George scoffed. "I thought he was sort of stupid."

"So did I," Bess added. "Why, he's probably lived at Mougarstown all his life, but he couldn't tell us much about the ranch country."

"I know," Nancy agreed with a slight frown. "But he doesn't pretend to be a rancher. He runs a book store."

"Then his interest in us is probably purely commercial," Bess insisted. "Maybe he thinks we'll buy books from him after we get to the ranch."

Nancy shook her head.

"I'm sure such a thing never entered his mind. He's just the quiet type. I can't help thinking that he's sorely troubled about something. He has such a tragic expression in his eyes."

"I didn't notice it myself." Bess declared. "Anyway, it's none of our concern. We'll probably never see him again after we reach our destination."

While the three girls had been discussing the stranger, Alice Regor had remained silent, but now she gave her opinion.

"I hope we do see him again. I like him— a lot."

"Someone stands up for me!" Nancy announced triumphantly.

However, as George and Bess continued to tease her about her interest in Ross Rogers, she did not bring up the subject again. At luncheon she found herself searching the dining car for the man, but he did not put in his appearance. Later in the day she met him in the observation car, but though he sat down beside her he said only a few words and then fell silent.

"I'm sure he isn't stupid as George seems to think," Nancy told herself. "And yet he does seem to be wrapped up in his own shell. Perhaps if I get the opportunity, I'll make a few inquiries about him when I get to Mougarstown."

CHAPTER III

The Journey's End

"Only fifteen more minutes, girls, and we'll be there!" George Fayne glanced at her wrist watch as she spoke and then out the window of the swift-moving train. "The country looks a little barren here, doesn't it?"

"A little!" Mrs. Rawley, who was putting on her hat and shaking the dust from her traveling suit, gave an amused little laugh. "It's positively forlorn. I had no idea it was as bad as this or I would never have come. This dry hot air will ruin my complexion."

"What do you care?" George scoffed. "I think a few freckles would be vastly becoming to you myself, Aunt Nell."

"Freckles! At my age! The very idea."

"I'm sure it will be cool and pleasant in the mountains," Nancy said optimistically.

"Well, I certainly hope so," Mrs. Rawley sighed. "At least it will be a relief to get off this stuffy train. It seems to me we've been riding a week."

"By the way, what's become of your friend,

Nancy?'' George demanded suddenly. ''I haven't seen him all day.''

''My friend?''

''Oh, you needn't pretend you don't know whom I mean. That Ross Rogers.''

''I haven't been keeping track of him.''

''But doesn't he get off at this next station?''

''I believe he does, George. He said he was going to Mougarstown, so he'll probably get off at the same station we do. I wish I could have said good-bye to him, but haven't seen him all afternoon. He's as shy as our Alice here.''

''I'm not shy,'' Alice defended herself. ''I just can't think of things to say.''

''I was only teasing,'' Nancy assured her quickly. ''The rest of us talk too much anyway.''

The conversation came to an abrupt end as the porter entered the car to warn the girls that their stop was the next one. They hastily began to gather together their baggage. Altogether there were twelve bags, to say nothing of the two trunks in the express car, and it made a staggering accumulation in the aisles.

''I hope they have a truck here to meet us!'' Nancy gasped.

A long, drawn out whistle warned them that they were approaching the station and a moment later the heavy train slowed down and came to a stop.

"Where's the station?" George demanded, glancing out of the window. "Why, we're still out in the prairie!"

"Come on!" Nancy cried, grabbing her by the arm. "Do you want to be left? The train stops here only a minute, the porter said."

The twelve bags had already been set off and Mrs. Rawley and the four girls quickly alighted. So interested were they in their surroundings that they failed to notice Ross Rogers swing from the train just before it started.

"My word!" Bess exclaimed. "Where is the town?"

"And where is the man that was to meet us?" Mrs. Rawley wailed.

"Perhaps we got off at the wrong station," Alice suggested timidly.

"That couldn't be," Nancy said quietly.

At this moment Ross Rogers, who had observed that something was amiss, came up and politely tipped his hat.

"Can I be of any assistance?"

"We were expecting someone to meet us and take us to Shadow Ranch," Mrs. Rawley explained. "It begins to look as though we're stranded. I was told there was a town here."

"The town is about a mile away, Madam. Undoubtedly, the man you were expecting has been delayed on the road. Can't I take your baggage into the station where you can wait?"

"Oh, thank you. Perhaps I can telephone to Shadow Ranch."

"I am sure your man will be along soon. The roads in this vicinity are not of the best and the car may have broken down."

With the girls helping him, Ross Rogers carried the bags into the little station and set them down near the door. The two trunks remained on the platform, forlorn and unwanted.

George gave one of them a disdainful kick with her boot.

"Whatever possessed me to bring that silly thing along? For two cents I'd put it on the track and get rid of it by letting a train run over it!"

"Thank you so much for helping us," Mrs. Rawley was saying to Ross Rogers. She hesitated and then added with a pleasant smile: "I do hope you'll visit us at Shadow Ranch sometime soon."

"I should like to."

After seeing that the girls were as comfortably settled as possible, Mr. Rogers said goodbye and started off on foot toward the town.

"Nice of him to help us with our baggage," Mrs. Rawley remarked. "I really hope he visits the ranch sometime, but I don't suppose he ever will as it's fifteen miles from here."

"It doesn't look as though we're going to get there ourselves," Bess declared soberly.

"What could have happened to that man who was to meet us?"

"Perhaps he didn't get your letter, Aunt Nell," George suggested.

"I sent it three weeks ago. I can't believe it went astray." As she spoke, she unthinkingly drew a pattern on the dusty wall and then in dismay looked at her grimy finger. "I don't believe this place has been disturbed in the last twenty years!"

Nancy, who had been standing at the window, now observed a dilapidated car draw up near the station platform and come to a wheezing halt. A lanky, gangling fellow in ill-fitting clothes slowly extracted himself from behind the steering wheel. Seeing the two trunks on the platform his jaw dropped and he stared blankly at them.

"I think the man we are looking for has arrived," Nancy announced.

The girls rushed out to meet the stranger, Mrs. Rawley following at a more dignified pace. The man stared curiously at the girls but offered no word of greeting.

"Are you Mrs. Rawley, the new owner of Shadder Ranch?" he demanded gruffly.

"Why, yes, I am," Mrs. Rawley returned, with her cordial smile.

"I'm George Miller," the man said, melting a trifle now that he saw the new ranch owner had no intention of "high toning" him. "If you'll jest step into the gas buggy here, I'll drive you to the ranch."

"How about the baggage?"

"We kin take some of the bags on the runnin' board. I'll have to send the wagon and mules for the rest of 'em and them two trunks."

"And now I must introduce my girls, Mr. Miller."

As Mrs. Rawley mentioned each one by name, George muttered a "pleased to meet you" and twisted his tattered felt hat with anguished hands. However, when George Fayne was introduced his shyness left him and he stared at the girl almost hostilely.

"George! George!" he growled. "That ain't no name for a gal!"

"It is my name though," George told him. "It's not even short for Georgia. Every one had given up hope for a boy in our family by the time I came, so I was named George, just plain George, for my grandfather."

"Grandfather dead at the time, I s'pose?"

"Why, yes," said George. "Why?"

"I knowed the man couldn't help himself!"

For a moment the two Georges glared at each other, and then both relaxed into grins. It was obvious to the others that in spite of their barbed words, the pair had taken to each other.

"Jest load yourselves in and we'll set off," the driver ordered. "Got a long rough road ahead of us."

The four girls climbed into the rear seat while Mrs. Rawley took the place beside George Miller. After some coaxing, the flivver started, and as George stepped on the gas it leaped away like a frisky young jack rabbit.

They drove to Mougarstown, where George stopped to buy groceries, and were surprised to learn that the place boasted a population of nearly a thousand persons. After the groceries had been loaded into the car, they took a narrow, rutty road leading north toward the mountains.

Though the girls tried not to show it, they were beginning to feel a little disappointed. So far they had viewed nothing but dry, barren country and whenever they passed another vehicle on the road, great clouds of dust rolled up and all but smothered them. Only the mountains in the distance offered a ray of hope.

As they drove along, Mrs. Rawley questioned George Miller about the ranch, inquiring the number of horses and cattle on the place as well as the condition of the various buildings. He answered the questions willingly enough and looked at the woman with new respect as she showed a keen appreciation of the situation.

"You aimin' to sell the place?" he asked after a time.

"I don't know what I shall do yet," Mrs. Rawley told him. "I can't tell until after I've seen the place."

"Shadder Ranch has run down considerable in the last few years," the driver said apologetically, "but it's still a blamed good ranch. I'd hate to see you sell 'er."

After that he relapsed into silence, and Mrs. Rawley and the girls were so tired that they did not take up the conversation.

Presently, the little car turned into a winding side road which led through the woods. As a breath of cool air struck the girls, their spirits revived and they began to observe their surroundings with new interest.

"This is more like it," Nancy declared.

In a few minutes the car emerged from the forest into a little clearing and then, plunging into another dense wood, crept down an incline so steep that the girls had to brace themselves to maintain their seats. They glanced uneasily at each other and wondered where in the world they were being taken. As they bumped over small stones and deep ruts, it seemed that they must be descending the side of a very steep mountain.

"Mountain?" George Miller grunted in response to their questions. "We ain't come to the mountain yet. This is jest a little hill.''

But at last the car turned a sharp corner and came to a groaning halt beside a huge boulder. With a sweep of his hand, George indicated the valley below.

"There you are, ladies.   That's Shadder Ranch.''

There was a quick intaking of breath and for a full minute the girls did not say a word. They simply stared in amazement at the grand panorama which was spread out before them. Below, there stretched a smooth carpet of rich green pasture land, and almost at the back door of the ranch a mountain rose up to meet the sky.   Never before had the girls viewed such a splendid scene, or such a dazzling array of colors.

"Oh, how perfectly lovely!'' Mrs. Rawley breathed at last. "After all, I'm glad I came.''

"I thought you'd like it,'' the driver declared, showing more enthusiasm than he had at any time during the drive.   He turned and winked at the girls.   "This ain't nothin' yet. Wait until you see the broncoes.   They're jest waitin' for some purty gals to ride 'em!''

CHAPTER IV

An Initial Adventure

The sight of Shadow Ranch, nestled at the base of the mountain, aroused the whole-hearted enthusiasm of Nancy Drew and her friends. Forgetting that they had ever been tired or discouraged, they fell to chattering like magpies. The instant the overburdened little car came to a halt in front of the old ranch house, they sprang eagerly to the ground.

Nancy surveyed her surroundings with keen interest. The ranch house was run-down and sadly in need of paint, but it was large and looked cool and inviting. Behind the house she caught a glimpse of the corrals and barns.

"I don't care if the place isn't in apple-pie order," she thought, "it's the most picturesque ranch imaginable."

As the driver led the way into the house, a stout woman, pleasant-faced and smiling, came out of the kitchen wiping her hands on her apron. George introduced her as his wife and she bowed self-consciously to Mrs. Rawley and the girls.

"Supper's most ready," she announced. "You'll just have time to go to your rooms and wash up."

The girls lost no time in following her suggestion, for the odor of hot biscuits, chicken sizzling in butter, and fragrant coffee, reminded them that they were hungry. Nancy Drew and George Fayne had been given a room together on the first floor while the others were to be quartered on the floor above.

"Well, how do you like it?" George demanded when they were together.

"Oh, I'm crazy about it already."

"So am I. Mrs. Miller is a dear."

"Hubby isn't so bad either, though as a foreman he'll never set the world on fire."

"He seems obsessed with the idea that George isn't any name for a girl. I heard him complaining about it to his wife only a few minutes ago."

"What do you care?"

"Oh, I don't," George laughed indifferently. "Still, I intend to make him like it before the summer is over!"

By the time they had freshened up a bit, the supper bell rang. With the others, Nancy and George sat down to a table which fairly groaned with plain but delicious food. They were served by Mrs. Miller who bustled about urging everyone to "eat hearty." The five cowboys em-

ployed on the ranch did not take supper with
Nancy and her friends, but came in after the
meal was finished to meet Mrs. Rawley and
the girls.

"Not one of them is under forty years of
age!" Bess complained in an undertone to
Nancy as they all went outdoors to inspect
the barns and stock. "Oh, why couldn't one
have been young and handsome?"

"Cheer up, Bess. You may find your hero
yet." Nancy turned to the foreman. "Where
are those broncoes you were telling us about?"

"Right this way. We've had to sell most
of our string, but we still have a few good
ponies left."

"Any tame ones?" Alice asked timidly.

The foreman might have laughed, but instead he replied soberly:

"Old Maud's just the hoss for you. She
wouldn't hurt a kitten."

"That's the kind I'm looking for, too," Bess
put in.

"Say, don't none of you know how to ride?"

"Nancy does," George declared.

"I can ride a little, but I'm no expert,"
Nancy insisted modestly.

"Then we'll jest turn this here ranch into a
riding school. By the time you go back to the
city you'll all be ready to join the rodeo circus."

"When do we take our first lesson?" George demanded eagerly.

"Well, say to-morrow mornin'."

"That suits me fine," George returned. "At what time?"

"Oh, say right after breakfast. About five-thirty."

"Five-thirty!" the girls echoed.

"Sure," Mr. Miller grinned. "I got work to do and that's the only time I can give you the benefit of my valuable instructions."

"I can get up by that hour if the rest of you can," Nancy said.

"I suppose I can too, if someone will pull me out," George grumbled.

And so it was decided that the girls were to take their first riding lesson the following morning. It seemed to Nancy that she had scarcely tumbled into bed when the alarm clock was warning her that it was time to get up. She rolled over and nudged George in the back, but that sleepy girl merely groaned and buried her head in the covers.

"Come on, lazy!" Nancy cried, pulling her out of bed.

"I've decided to wait until to-morrow morning," George pleaded.

"Not much you haven't! Come on out, young lady!"

Nancy and George were the first to appear at the corrals, but very shortly Alice and Bess came up. Mr. Miller had already saddled four ponies and led them up to where the girls were standing. As one of the animals took a playful nip at Bess's shoulder she promptly backed away and climbed the fence. The foreman gave a grunt of disgust.

"Here, Miss Drew," he said, giving Nancy the bridle of the most spirited pony. "This hoss is kind o' temperamental but if you handle her right she won't give you any trouble."

Nancy vaulted lightly into the saddle, and the foreman nodded in approval as he saw that she was well able to take care of herself.

Bess next tried to mount the pony which had been turned over to her but at her first attempt, the animal shied away.

"Say, didn't no one ever tell you to git on a hoss from the left side?" Mr. Miller berated her.

Guiltily, Bess changed sides, but her second attempt was no more successful than the first. Her foot caught in the stirrup and she could neither extract it nor raise herself to the saddle. To the amusement of the cowboys who had perched themselves on the fence to watch the fun, the horse began to move slowly away, and Bess, hopping along on one foot, began to cry frantically: "Whoa! Whoa!"

Rescued from this predicament, she insisted
upon backing the horse up to the fence and
mounting from there. Alice followed her example, but George, though somewhat lacking
in grace, managed to vault into the saddle without assistance.

As Bess later described it to her aunt, the
lesson proceeded from bump to bump. Mr.
Miller made the girls trot their ponies around
the corral until they felt that all of their bones
had been jolted from their bodies. Yet, by
the end of the lesson George had caught the
knack of posting and Alice was rapidly im-
proving.

"I'd have done better," Bess apologized,
"but I had to hang on to the saddle so hard I
couldn't concentrate on what the pony was going to do next."

"I guess we'll have to let Nancy take all
the honors," George sighed. "She's a regular
whiz at it."

While Nancy Drew had never taken many
riding lessons, it was true that she sat her
horse well and rode with confidence and ease.
The cowboys had watched her admiringly as
she galloped about the field.

"When do we take the next lesson?" George
asked the foreman after the ponies had been
led away. "To-morrow?"

"Unless I miss my guess, you gals won't be

feelin' much like ridin' to-morrow," he laughed.

To their sorrow, the girls found that Mr. Miller was correct. On the morrow they were in no condition for riding, but by the following day all stiffness had worn away, and they were again eager for another lesson.

At first the girls did not dare venture far from the ranch in their daily rides, but as they became more skillful in handling their ponies, they gradually increased the distance. Even Bess Marvin came to look forward to the lessons, though a number of tumbles served to remind her in an unpleasant way that she had not improved as rapidly as the others. At last, Mr. Miller announced that there were to be no more lessons.

"You mean we're experts at last?" George demanded.

"Well, I wouldn't go so far as to say that," the foreman returned truthfully. "But you've learned enough to take care of yourselves. You can ride wherever you like now."

"Anywhere?" Nancy questioned eagerly. "Then I want to go up into the mountains."

"I guess it will be safe enough if you take a guide. I can spare Jack Glenwell to-morrow if you want to go then."

"Let's make it an all-day picnic," Nancy proposed.

The others enthusiastically agreed and fell

to outlining their plans. At the suggestion of
Jack Glenwell, one of the punchers, it was decided that they would take the Big Bear Creek
trail, a very scenic bridle path leading fifteen
miles up into the mountains. Consulting Mrs.
Miller, they found her more than willing to
prepare a picnic luncheon.

"I wish Aunt Nell could go with us," Alice
said, as they were talking over the plans. "It
doesn't seem fair for us to have all the fun."

"Aunt Nell wouldn't call a fifteen mile ride
any fun," George told her. "She hates horseback riding, and, anyway, she has her hands
full trying to straighten out things here at the
ranch."

Early the next morning, the four girls were
astir. After a hearty breakfast of bacon and
eggs and Mrs. Miller's good coffee, they
mounted their ponies, and, with Jack Glenwell
in the lead, set off for the mountains. Mrs.
Rawley waved her handkerchief until they were
out of sight.

"It's a splendid day for riding," Nancy
Drew remarked to the guide.

"Yes," Jack Glenwell replied with a glance
at the sky. "Still, I can't say that I like the
looks of those clouds over to the southwest.
Storms come up here pretty quick sometimes."

Nancy cast a quick glance in the direction
indicated but to her the clouds did not appear

threatening. The sun was beating down as brightly and as hot as ever.

"You don't really think it will rain, do you?" she asked anxiously.

"Oh, probably not before we get back," the guide assured her easily.

Nancy's fears were set at rest. Forgetting the weather entirely, she was soon absorbed in the beauty of the mountain scenery. Jack Glenwell led the way along a steep, rocky path which followed Big Bear Creek. The girls halted occasionally to gaze at a waterfall or to permit their ponies to drink at the stream. They breathed deeply of the fresh mountain air, and were grateful for the dense canopy of trees which shaded them from the scorching rays of the sun.

"Say, girls, when do we eat?" Bess called out at last. "I'm about starved."

"Why not stop here?" Nancy suggested. "I see a big flat rock where we can spread out our luncheon."

While Jack Glenwell looked after the ponies, the girls laid out the picnic things, and everything was in readiness when the guide returned. However, instead of accepting the plate of food which had been prepared for him, he called Nancy aside.

"I don't want to alarm the others," he told her quietly, "but there's a bad storm coming

up. We'll have to call off the rest of our trip.
I think it's wisest to eat just as quickly as we
can and start for the ranch."

Nancy looked upward but could not see the
sky because of the dense foliage. She nodded
soberly.

"We'll get started just as soon as we can."

Luncheon was dispatched with speed, and
as soon as everyone had finished eating, Nancy
told the girls that they must start immediately
for the ranch. This announcement was greeted
with a chorus of protest, which quickly sub-
sided when Jack Glenwell explained that a
storm was closing in upon them.

"What if it does rain a little?" George demanded. "I'm sure I wouldn't mind a little
wetting."

"You don't know these mountain storms,"
the guide told her tersely.

The sober look on the man's face was enough
to convince the girls that there was genuine
cause for alarm. Hastily, they gathered up
the picnic things and mounted their ponies.

"We must hurry right along," the guide
said as they started off, "or we'll never
make it."

Even as he spoke, Nancy felt the first light
drop of rain upon her hand. Urging her pony
faster, she glanced apprehensively about her.
Almost in an instant, it seemed, darkness had

dropped like a shroud upon the mountain trail. A cold blast of air stirred the leaves of the trees, whispering an ominous warning of the approaching storm.

"Oh, dear, I wish we hadn't come," Bess wailed.

Nancy felt another drop of rain upon her hand. Soon there was a steady rustle overhead.

"We're in for it," Jack Glenwell muttered.

At first the leaves partially protected the riders, but all at once the very clouds seemed to open and a deluge came pouring down upon their heads.

"Oh, can't we stop?" Alice begged. "I can't see where I'm going."

"We must keep going," the guide insisted. "You don't know these storms the way I do. We must get back to Big Bear Creek and ford it before the flood waters strand us on the mountain."

On down the slippery trail they rode, wondering if Jack Glenwell was not exaggerating the danger. Yet, as the minutes passed and still the rain did not show the slightest sign of letting up, they began to realize that a mountain storm was not to be taken lightly.

The rain pelted into their faces, half blinding them. The wind tore at them. The ponies,

heads down, almost on their haunches, slid and
sidled down the steep grade. At one particularly steep place, Alice Regor lost her balance
and slipped sideways from the saddle. Just
before she fell entirely from the pony Jack
Glenwell rode hastily to her side and caught
hold of her.

"Keep your feet in the stirrups," he said
sharply. "If you stick to your pony you'll be
all right," he added more gently.

Thoroughly drenched and uncomfortable, it
seemed to Nancy Drew and her friends that
they would never reach the creek. They dared
not urge their ponies faster, for the path was
dangerously steep and slippery.

"We're almost there," the guide encouraged
them after a time. He halted his pony and
listened intently.

Nancy, too, stopped in the trail. To her horror, she distinctly heard the sound of rushing
torrents of water.

"Come on!" the guide shouted. "We may
be too late now to make it!"

Of one accord the girls urged their ponies
into a gallop. At a reckless speed they plunged
down the slope toward the creek. Emerging
from the wood, they came into view of the
stream and stopped in amazement. There before them was Big Bear Creek, but from a list-

less little stream it had been transformed to a raging torrent, and at each moment the water was rising higher.

"Oh, what shall we do?" Bess cried.

"I believe we can still make it!" Jack told the girls. "Are you game to try?"

"It's our only chance of getting back to the ranch," Nancy added quickly.

"I'm not afraid," George said quietly.

"I'll try it," Alice announced, but her face was white.

Bess nodded grimly.

"Then come on! I'll go first and if I make it, you girls follow."

Whipping up his horse, the guide plunged boldly into the stream, leaving Nancy and her friends to hold their breath in fear. It seemed that both horse and rider must certainly be swept down with the current, but though the flood waters surged up as far as Jack's boots it came no higher. He reached the opposite bank in safety.

"You can make it!" he called back. "Hurry!"

George and Alice had already started the perilous trip, and with Jack encouraging them from the opposite shore they made the trip without mishap.

"Come on, Bess!" Nancy commanded.

Bess stared at the racing water with horror in her eyes.

"I can't do it," she wailed, for her courage had left her at the last minute.

"Nonsense!" Nancy told her sharply. "Don't be a coward! Go on! There isn't a minute to lose!"

When George and Alice had accomplished the ford, Nancy had not failed to notice that the water had covered the girls' knees. Each moment that they delayed only increased the danger.

"You go first, Nancy," Bess pleaded.

Nancy shook her head.

"Go on!" she cried again.

Bess gave her pony a slap on the flank and steeled herself for the plunge. Nancy, watching her anxiously, saw her reach the middle of the stream in safety. Then, as the waters crept higher and higher about the frightened girl, she instinctively tightened her hold upon the reins. The pony stopped short and would not go on. To the horror-stricken spectators on either side of the shore, it appeared almost certain that both horse and rider were doomed, for Bess, in her terror, made no effort to control her mount.

"Save me!" she cried, clinging helplessly to the saddle. "Oh, save me!"

CHAPTER V

REFUGE

EVEN as Nancy Drew realized that Bess Marvin was in grave danger, she urged her pony toward the turbulent stream, calling out a word of encouragement to the frightened girl. At first Nancy's frightened pony whirled, refusing to enter the boisterous water. Then the girl gained the mastery and forced the animal first to the edge of the stream and then into the rushing flood of waters. As the swift current caught her in its embrace, she gritted her teeth and gave her mount free rein. Could she reach Bess or would she too be washed downstream?

On the opposite shore George Fayne and the guide were shouting frantic advice to Bess, but in her dazed state it was doubtful if she even heard. She continued to cling helplessly to the saddle, while her pony wavered uncertainly.

Then Nancy reached her and clutched the bridle. The pony jerked up its head, striking Bess in the face. For a moment it appeared to those on the shore that both girls were to be swept downstream. But Nancy's pony was sure of foot and was now under perfect control and faltered for the instant only.

On Nancy came, leading Bess's pony. Both reached safety, and poor Bess, half dead with fright, was lifted to the ground by Jack Glenwell.

"Oh, I never was so frightened in all my life!" Bess murmured brokenly. "When I saw all that water surging about me, I got dizzy and I couldn't think what I was doing."

"Don't think about it," Nancy advised kindly. "You're all right now."

"You saved me, Nancy."

"All I did was to grab hold of the bridle. You would have been all right if you hadn't become frightened."

"This creek is rising fast," the guide interrupted. "In a few minutes it will be flooding the banks. We'd better get away while we can."

"Isn't there a house near by where we can wait until the rain is over?" Nancy asked. "We'll all catch bad colds if we ride to the ranch in wet clothing."

The guide hesitated.

"There's a cottage about a quarter of a mile from here."

"There's no danger of the flood extending that far?"

"Not unless it rains for several hours."

"Then why can't we go there?"

"Well, I suppose we can," the guide said slowly, "though I don't know what sort of a welcome we'll get. You see, an old woman lives there and she's sort of queer. Martha Frank is her name."

"If she'll let us in, that's all we care," Nancy declared. "Lead the way."

The girls hastily mounted again and followed the guide on down the trail. Presently they came to a dilapidated shack which was set back in the woods, and there drew rein.

"Not much of a mansion," Jack assured them.

"We can at least get warm," Alice chattered.

As there was no barn or out building, the guide tied the ponies to a tree and then the five made their way to the cottage. Jack rapped sharply on the door. There was no response.

"I'm sure I heard someone inside," Nancy insisted.

The guide knocked again, so loudly that the door rattled.

"I can hear someone coming now," Bess whispered.

The words were scarcely out of her mouth when the door was cautiously opened by an old woman with wispy gray hair and sharp, black eyes. She gazed upon the five with undisguised distrust but not a word did she speak.

The guide explained that his party had been caught in the storm and were looking for a refuge. The old woman listened intently and kept peering first at one of the girls and then at another, but still not a sound escaped her.

"May we come in?" Jack asked, a trifle impatiently.

For answer, the woman moved aside and opened the door. The girls filed in, grateful for the shelter, even though it were grudgingly offered.

"What can be the matter with that woman?" George whispered to Nancy. "Has she lost her voice?"

The room into which the girls were ushered was nearly destitute of furniture. There were a few chairs, a table, a cot and a cookstove, but the floor and walls were bare. Apparently, the cottage consisted of only two rooms. Nancy glanced curiously toward the bedroom and was somewhat embarrassed when Martha Frank, following her glance, moved over and closed the door.

"How about a little fire?" the guide asked the old woman, after several painful minutes of silence had elapsed. "If we could dry our clothing——"

Without a word the woman got up from her chair and began to throw a few sticks of wood into the cookstove. Jack went over to help her.

"I wish we hadn't come," Alice whispered to Nancy. "That woman has such cruel eyes."

Nancy did not reply, for just then she was startled to see the door of the bedroom open a crack. As she watched, the crack widened, and then to her astonishment a girl of perhaps eleven or twelve stepped out into the room. Though dressed in the ugliest rags imaginable, the child was unusually pretty; she had almost prefect features and her curly golden hair would have been lovely had it been properly washed. The girl's face was thin and she looked undernourished. Nancy's heart went out to her at once, for it seemed a pity that such an attractive child must live in such wretched circumstances. Obviously, Martha Frank gave her no care or attention.

As the child paused in the doorway, staring blankly at the strangers, the old woman wheeled and saw her.

"Lucy!" she snarled.

She spoke no other word, but a look of fear came over the child's face. She cringed and then, turning, rushed over to the door and ran outside into the rain.

"Oh, don't let her do that!" Nancy cried, getting up and hurrying to the door.

She looked out, but the child had vanished into the storm. Glancing toward Martha

Frank, she saw that the old woman had not
the slightest concern about what became of
the girl.

"Why don't you call her back?" Nancy demanded, a trifle sharply.

The old woman merely shrugged her
shoulders.

"I think we had better go," Nancy said with
decision. "If we do that child may come back.
It isn't right for us to drive her out into the
storm."

"Do let's go," Alice agreed quickly. "It's
nearly stopped raining anyway."

Thanking Martha Frank for the shelter, the
five hastily left the cottage. In the yard they
looked about, but the child was nowhere to be
seen. Mounting their ponies, they rode away.

Yet, as she rode swiftly toward Shadow
Ranch, Nancy continued to contemplate the
strange happenings of the afternoon. What
could it all mean? Who was this child called
Lucy and what relation could she be to Martha
Frank?

"I intend to ask Jack as soon as we get back
to the ranch," she told herself. "Perhaps he
can tell me what I want to know."

CHAPTER VI

NANCY INVESTIGATES

NANCY could not forget Martha Frank, and continued to reflect on the strange actions of the old woman and on her unlikeness in appearance to the child Lucy. However, it was not until the following day that she found an opportunity to draw Jack Glenwell aside and question him. The puncher was willing enough to tell her everything he knew, but unfortunately had little information to offer.

"No one seems to know much about Martha," he told Nancy. "She came here about seven years ago and just squatted on the place."

"The child is her own?"

"No, her name is Lucy Brown. Apparently, they're no relation to each other."

"I thought she didn't look anything like Martha Frank," Nancy commented thoughtfully. "A pretty little thing, isn't she?"

"Yes, the kid is all right, I guess, but no one seems to like the woman."

"Has she made trouble in the community?"

"No, she keeps entirely to herself; but her

attitude toward Lucy has aroused considerable antagonism.''

''How do you mean?''

''Oh, she neglects her.''

''Lets her run wild, I suppose?''

''On the contrary, she keeps her penned up like a prisoner. She doesn't give her enough to eat or wear, so folks say.''

''I should think the neighbors would interfere.''

''That's easier said than done. The old woman has a shotgun and, believe me, she knows how to use it! Folks just let her alone until Lucy was of school age. Then the school committee took a hand and threatened her with eviction if she didn't send her to school.''

''She gave in?''

''Yes, she couldn't help herself. She sent Lucy to school, but dressed her in rags and didn't even give her enough money to buy necessary supplies. Often she was sent to school without any lunch.''

''Why, that's dreadful!''

''The school authorities talked with her several times and she always promised to do better and never did.''

''How was Lucy in her school work?''

''They say she was as bright as any of them, but that only made it harder for her to make friends. The other children taunted her about being a squatter and wouldn't have anything to do with her.''

''I suppose not,'' Nancy said musingly. ''Tell me, how does Martha Frank manage to live?''

''That's a poser all right. She works a little garden and it probably doesn't take much to keep just the two of them.''

''But surely she couldn't manage on the garden alone. She must have some money.''

''Oh, I guess she has a little—enough to buy meat and staples.''

''You don't know where she lived before she came here?''

Jack Glenwell shook his head.

''I never heard and I doubt if anyone knows.'' He glanced curiously at Nancy. ''Why this particular interest in Martha, anyway?''

''Oh, I'm not especially interested in her,'' Nancy returned hastily. ''It was Lucy I was thinking about. It seems to me something should to be done for her. Martha Frank has no right to mistreat her.''

''She ought to be forced to give up the girl,'' the puncher agreed.

''I wonder if she is Lucy's legal guardian?''

''You've got me there.''

As the puncher had told Nancy all that he knew, the girl thanked him for the information and turned away. However, she was by no

means satisfied that she had learned everything there was to know about Martha Frank.
She felt certain that Lucy Brown came of far
better stock than squatter quality. What could
be the tie that bound her to Martha? Obviously,
they had no affection for each other and the
child had appeared actually to fear the old
woman.

"I wish I could have talked with Lucy,"
Nancy mused. "I can't help being interested in
her. Poor thing! She's badly in need of a
friend!"

Her thoughts were interrupted as George and
Bess came out of the ranch house looking for
her. Though Bess had caught a slight cold, the
girls appeared none the worse for their adventure of the previous day. One might have
thought that their unfortunate experience would
have dampened their enthusiasm for riding,
but such was not the case. Even Bess had announced that she did not intend to give up.

"Where's Alice?" Nancy greeted the girls.

"In the house," George returned. "I asked
her if she didn't want to go with us on a hike,
but she said no."

"Is she ill?" Nancy inquired anxiously, for
she knew that Alice was not as strong as the
others.

"No, I guess she just wants to be alone,"
Bess replied.

"I hope it wasn't that trip into the mountains——"

"Oh, no, it isn't that," Bess told her. "She wasn't half as frightened as I was and she didn't even catch a cold."

"If you ask me, I'd say it's just another siege of the blues," George declared, lowering her voice lest it carry into the ranch house.

"She's worrying about her father again?"

George nodded.

"That's what I think, though she won't tell me a thing. She just bottles her trouble up inside of her and it makes her dreadfully unhappy."

"I feel so sorry for her."

"So do I," Bess agreed, "but there's nothing we can do about it." Abruptly she changed the subject. "Do you feel like hiking this morning?"

Nancy hesitated and then shook her head.

"You girls go on without me. I think I'll just loaf around the ranch house for a while."

She stood at the fence and watched Bess and George until they were out of sight, and then, turning abruptly, went into the house. After a moment of indecision, she climbed the stairs to the second floor and knocked quietly on Alice Regor's door. At first there was no response and Nancy was about to turn away when she heard a muffled, "come in."

Entering, she saw at a glance that Alice had been crying.

"Oh, I didn't mean to intrude," Nancy apologized quickly.

"Don't go," Alice said. "I—I guess I need someone to cheer me up."

"I'm a grand little optimist," Nancy smiled, as she sat down on the bed. "What seems to be wrong, Alice?"

"Oh, everything! I'm so unhappy. If only—" She checked herself suddenly.

"If only what?" Nancy asked gently. "Don't be afraid to tell me."

"I was going to say, if only father hadn't gone away. Oh, Nancy!" She flung out her hands in a gesture of despair. "Everyone said he ran away and left Mother and me, but I know he didn't! I just know it!"

"I'm sure he didn't," Nancy agreed comfortingly. "I've already heard something of the story, so you needn't tell me about it. I understand."

"I wanted you to know," Alice said simply. "I don't mean to let it affect me, but I can't help it."

"I wish I could help you, Alice."

"I'm afraid no one can do that, Nancy. Some day father will come back and then everything will be right again."

Alice got up from the bed and going over

to the dresser began to dab powder on her nose. She turned again to Nancy and tried to smile.

"I'm over the weeps now, I guess. Do I look a sight?"

"Not in the least," Nancy assured her.

Alice gave her hair a few pats and then the girls went downstairs together, to sit with Mrs. Rawley on the veranda. After a time Alice picked up a book and began to read but Nancy, who frequently looked her way, noticed that she seldom turned a page.

A faraway expression had crept into her eyes and it told Nancy more plainly than words that the girl was still brooding over her trouble. She had only pretended to shake off the mood of despondency.

"Her entire vacation will be ruined," Nancy told herself. "If only I could think of something that would help her to forget!"

CHAPTER VII

THE ROUND-UP

NANCY had made up her mind to think of some diversion which would help poor Alice forget her great trouble, but as chance had it, she was not called upon to do so, for the very next day Mrs. Rawley made an announcement which served her own purpose admirably.

The girls were seated at the breakfast table when Mrs. Rawley first mentioned her plan. The conversation had begun with a casual discussion of the ranch work which must be accomplished before her return to the East.

"I hope to sell the ranch eventually," she explained, "but so far I've been unable to find a buyer. I suppose I can't expect to get my price unless I make certain repairs."

"You expect to remodel?" Nancy inquired.

"I've considered it from every angle and I believe it will save money in the end. The barn is about ready to fall down and there isn't a decent fence on the place."

"You'll not be able to clear up the work for several weeks then?" George asked, trying not to show her eagerness for a negative answer.

"I'm afraid not." Mrs. Rawley lowered her voice so that it would not reach Mrs. Miller who was busy in the kitchen. "I know Mr. Miller has done the best he can, but he just isn't a manager. It seems to me that the best thing to do is to sell some of the steers and use the money from their sale to make the necessary repairs. Then I should be able to dispose of the ranch without difficulty."

"It sounds like a sensible plan to me," Nancy observed. "Will you have any trouble selling the steers?"

"No, I'll take the market on them, which happens to be especially attractive at this time. The only thing is that I must arrange to ship without delay. That will mean a round-up."

"A round-up?" Nancy cried eagerly.

"Oh, man!" George exclaimed enthusiastically, forgetting that her aunt frowned upon slang. "I never thought I'd get to see a real round-up!"

"It can't be a very large one, because there aren't many steers on the range. Of course, the round-ups of the old days are gone forever, but we'll have a sample of what they were like."

"We don't care if it is only a miniature round-up," Nancy declared. "It will be the real thing and not a moving picture of something that never happened.''

As she spoke she glanced toward Alice and was gratified to see that the girl's face had lighted up with interest.

"Will the men let us help, do you suppose?" Nancy asked hopefully. "It would be fun to be one of the riders."

"I'll speak to Mr. Miller about it. He says you are all getting to be experts and I know we'll have to have extra help."

"I'm sure Mr. Miller wasn't thinking of me when he said that," Bess said with a sigh. "If we have a round-up I'll be relegated to the fence."

"Would you like to ride if Mr. Miller will let us?" Nancy asked, turning to Alice.

"Indeed I would," Alice replied quickly with more enthusiasm than she had shown for many days. "I think it would be heaps of fun."

"Let's go find Mr. Miller now and ask him if we may," George proposed, pushing back her chair.

The four girls rushed out of the ranch house, Mrs. Rawley following at a more moderate pace. They found the foreman at the corrals and Mrs. Rawley quickly explained her plan.

"I reckon we can have a general round-up in a couple of days," he told her; "but we'll have to get two or three riders from the Bar X Ranch.''

''The girls were saying that they wished they might help.''

''Well, why not?'' the foreman demanded gruffly. ''Course they couldn't do the branding or the bulldogging, but they could help herd.''

''They wouldn't be in any danger, would they?'' Mrs. Rawley asked.

''Not a mite as long as they stuck in the saddle. Course if they fell off into a herd of cattle——''

''I don't believe I want to ride,'' Bess said hastily. ''I think I'd rather watch.''

''Well, I wouldn't,'' George announced. ''You may count me as one of the riders.''

''All right, Miss Fayne, but I warn you it will be hard work.'' The foreman bestowed a provoking grin upon George and pronounced her name with an accent on the ''Fayne.'' From the first he had steadily refused to call her George, although he addressed the others by their first names.

''I want to ride too!'' Nancy declared. ''I wouldn't miss it for anything!''

''Neither would I,'' Alice said.

''Then it's all decided,'' Mrs. Rawley announced as she turned toward the house.

"We'll have the big round-up day after to-morrow."

"This won't be no big round-up," the foreman protested, quick to correct the Eastern lady who had shown such an aptitude for the ranching business. "It'll be more like drivin' home the cows."

"I was merely speaking figuratively," Mrs. Rawley laughed.

"There ain't been a regular round-up in this country for a good many years," the foreman said ruminatively. "Those were the days! All the boys would get together, and we'd be two weeks driving the cattle to the corrals. Things haven't been the same since they took the free range."

Though George Miller continued to make disparaging remarks about the coming round-up, the girls decided that most of them were for the purpose of impressing the new ranch owner. They noticed that he went about with a lighter step and was frequently whistling an old cowboy tune.

"I guess he is as thrilled about the round-up as anyone, but he doesn't want to show it," Nancy laughed.

She was well pleased at the effect which had been produced on Alice Regor. The girl had entered whole-heartedly into the plans, and for the time at least had forgotten her troubles.

On the morning set for the round-up the girls were abroad at four o'clock. Although Mrs. Miller had prepared an unusually hearty breakfast, they were too excited to do it justice. Hurrying out to the corrals, they found that one of the cowboys had already saddled their ponies.

"Better come along with us, Bess," George urged her cousin. "You'll miss a lot of fun."

Bess shook her head.

"I'd get a dreadful sunburn, and, anyway, if a big ugly steer came at me, I know I'd become panic stricken. No, I'd rather wait here and watch everything from a distance."

"We're ready to start," the foreman interrupted impatiently. He turned to Nancy. "I'm letting you ride Bonzo. She's a regular cow pony and can cut out with the best of them."

Nancy glanced uneasily at her new mount which obviously was far more spirited than the one she had been riding. However, she was determined not to show that she was afraid, and so sprang lightly into the saddle. In addition to the foreman there were six cowboys who were to ride, as one had been imported from the Bar X Ranch.

As George Miller gave the word, the little party clattered away in a cloud of dust, leaving

Bess and Mrs. Rawley to wave their handkerchiefs from the veranda. Reaching a little knoll perhaps a mile from the ranch, the foreman called a halt and gave his orders.

"Jack, you take Nancy and Miss Fayne. Pete can have Jim True and Alice. We'll drive the cattle toward this knoll."

The groups separated, Nancy and George going with Jack Glenwell and taking the eastern portion of the range. For several hours they kept to their saddles, but though the work was tiring, the girls did not complain. Jack explained that irrespective of brands, all cattle were to be driven toward the central point, and that such cutting out as was necessary would be done there.

"I didn't suppose the cattle still roamed free," Nancy commented.

"They don't, except as we have an agreement with the Bar X Ranch and let our cattle range with theirs. The Bar X brand is the only one we'll have to cut out."

"Hi, Nancy, look at that cow getting away!" yelled George Fayne.

But Nancy Drew had already seen and had turned and was away on a swift gallop after the straying steer. On she flew, trying to circle the ranging animal. At last she got around and rode forward to head the steer toward the rest of the herd.

"My, I wonder what the proper way to do this thing is," sighed Nancy to herself. "I guess I don't know much about driving steers."

Fortunately, Bonzo did know her business, and between that and Nancy Drew's general common sense the straying steer was driven back to the herd.

"Good work, Nancy," Jack Glenwell said to her, and she did not confess her own doubts as to her real ability in the work.

When noon came, Nancy and George ate their luncheon in the saddle that the work might not be delayed. By two o'clock they had rounded up the last stray cow and calf and were driving the herd toward the knoll.

"I wonder how Alice got along?" George remarked to Nancy. "I hope she had as much fun as we did."

After Jack Glenwell and the girls had joined the other riders, herding the cattle all together, Nancy, during a brief resting spell, caught a glimpse of Alice and rode over to her.

"Have any trouble?" she inquired.

"Not a bit," Alice returned with animation. "I wish we were having a round-up like this every day."

"So do I," Nancy said to herself. "I haven't seen Alice enjoying herself like this since she started for Arizona."

The two girls did not have an opportunity

to talk, for with the cattle herded, the work of
cutting out those belonging to the Bar X Ranch
was started. In this Nancy was permitted to
help, but Alice and George were content to
watch from the sidelines.

With the others, Nancy rode fearlessly into
the herd. Her mount was a trained cow pony
and almost by instinct, it seemed, ferreted out
the cows belonging to the Bar X Ranch, nipping
at their heels until they were driven from the
herd. If she was uneasy she did not show it,
working deliberately and with cool calculation.

Once she was in actual danger when an infuriated cow refused to leave the herd and instead charged upon Nancy's mount, horns
lowered angrily. With a snort of fright, Bonzo
reared into the air.

Nancy flung herself forward and managed to
retain her seat. She pulled the pony to her
four feet and was already out of the way of the
direct charge when two of the cowboys drove
through the herd to help her. The infuriated
cow was cut out from the group and Nancy went
on with her work as coolly as before. She had
learned that such situations were but ordinary
incidents in the career of a cowboy.

At last the cattle of the Bar X were separated
from those of Shadow Ranch and left to graze.
Those belonging to the Shadow Ranch were
driven toward the corrals.

As Nancy and the others rode up, Mrs. Rawley and Bess came out to the fence to watch.

"What are they going to do now?" Bess asked Nancy, as she noticed that one of the cowboys had started a fire not far from the corral.

"They must brand the calves before turning them back to pasture," Nancy explained.

"I don't think I want to watch that!"

Yet when the time came Bess Marvin did watch, and became even more excited than the others. From the safety of the fence the girls saw the cowboys wrestle with the calves, tie their legs together, and finally drag them to the branding irons.

It was long after sundown before the work was finished, and by that time the girls realized that they were dead tired. As soon as they had eaten their suppers they tumbled into bed and knew no more until Mrs. Miller rapped on their doors and told them it was time to get up.

"The men are driving the cattle to Mougarstown to-day," Mrs. Rawley told the girls at the breakfast table. "Any of you want to go to town?"

"We all do," George told her, answering for the others. "Are we to help drive?"

"If you like, but I would advise against it."

"It would just be an uncomfortable, dusty ride," Nancy declared.

"I was thinking we could all go in the car," Mrs. Rawley went on. "Mr. Miller can drive us over. Then after the cattle are loaded we can take in the picture show. Mrs. Miller tells me this is the regular night for it."

"It seems ages since I've seen a moving picture," Bess laughed.

"Don't worry!" George cut in. "You've probably seen this one. More than likely it's ten years old!"

"Let's go, anyway," Nancy said. "It will give us something to do."

Soon after luncheon the party set off in the little car, arriving at Mougarstown ahead of the herd which was being driven by the five cowboys. As Mrs. Rawley wished to watch the loading, they went to the stockyards over by the little railroad station, remaining there until the last car had been filled.

"I think I'll get them to market at exactly the right time," Mrs. Rawley remarked to the girls as they left the yards. "I should get a good price—better than I expected."

Mrs. Miller had asked the girls to purchase supplies for the ranch, and they now proceeded toward the town, a mile away, leaving Mrs. Rawley to attend to certain business matters at the freight station with the agent, who promised to drive her over to the town later.

As the girls walked slowly down the main

street Nancy caught sight of a stationery store and called the attention of the others to it.

"I wonder if Mr. Rogers doesn't own that place. Let's stop and see."

"Oh, why bother," George protested. "It's nearly five o'clock now and we'll just have time to buy the groceries before the stores close."

"This isn't the city," Nancy reminded her. "The stores will be open until ten o'clock."

"Well, anyway, Aunt Nell said we were to meet her at the car by nine o'clock. If we get supper and go to the first moving picture show we won't have any more than enough time."

"Oh, all right," Nancy gave in.

They bought the supplies for the ranch and carried them to the car. Going to a little restaurant which Mr. Miller had recommended, they ate their suppers and then started for the moving picture theater. However, before they had gone very far, Bess remembered that she had forgotten to mail a letter.

"The post office is two blocks back," George informed her cousin. "We'll wait here for you to return."

"I'll go along," Alice offered. "I want to get some stamps."

The two girls hurried off, leaving Nancy and George to wait for them.

"We may as well walk on," George suggested. "They'll catch up."

Accordingly, they moved slowly on down the street, frequently pausing to look in the store windows.

"What do you suppose is keeping Alice and that cousin of mine?" George asked presently, looking back over her shoulder. "They aren't even in——"

She broke off suddenly, as Nancy caught her by the wrist. Turning quickly, she saw that her friend was staring fixedly into an old junk shop.

"What is it?" George asked.

"Look in there!" Nancy whispered. "See that woman!"

"It's Martha Frank!"

"Yes, and something is the matter! Oh! I do believe she's going to strike that man!"

CHAPTER VIII

A QUARREL

NANCY DREW and George Fayne had no desire to pry into business which did not concern them, but as a loud clamor issued from within the old junk shop, they paused involuntarily and glanced that way. To their surprise they saw Martha Frank, the old woman of the mountain, engaged in a heated argument with a wizened little man, evidently the owner of the shop.

"I won't! I won't!" they heard Martha fairly scream. "If you threaten me I'll——"

She raised her arm as though to strike the man, but he caught her wrist and gave it a sharp wrench.

"You'll do as I say!" he told her angrily. "Now git out o' here! Do you want folks to see you?"

The old woman gave a startled glance toward the window. The fire seemed to have left her, for with a frightened look upon her face, she moved toward the door.

Nancy and George, suddenly aware of their position, hurried on.

"Imagine seeing Martha Frank in Mougars-town!" George exclaimed when they were a safe distance beyond the shop. "And in such a place! I wonder what she was so angry about?"

"That's what I'd like to know myself," Nancy commented dryly.

"Perhaps she was trying to get a good bargain."

"It didn't sound much like that to me. I heard her say, 'if you threaten me,' but she didn't finish the sentence."

"That's so. I was so amazed at hearing Martha speak that I didn't really register on what she was saying."

"I wonder whom she was quarreling with," Nancy mused thoughtfully. "I certainly wasn't favorably impressed with that man's appearance."

"Neither was I. He seemed to have some sort of hold over Martha, too, because when he told her to get out, she left without a word."

"I noticed that."

The conversation ended at this point as Alice and Bess came rushing up, slightly out of breath.

"We couldn't find the post office at first," Alice apologized. "That's why it took us so long."

"You'd never guess whom we met on the

street!'' Bess broke in eagerly. ''Martha Frank, and she was marching along like some-one had stepped on her pet corn!''

''She didn't even look at us,'' Alice added.

Nancy and George smiled knowingly.

''You girls missed the best part of it,'' George informed them importantly. ''She just had a quarrel with the junkman!''

Pressed for details, Nancy and George quickly related what they had overheard.

''She's a queer one all right,'' Bess commented. She glanced at her wrist watch. ''Say, we'll have to hurry if we're going to the first show. It's time for it to start this minute.''

Since they had promised to meet Mrs. Raw-ley at nine o'clock, the girls hurried on to the moving picture theater. The advertisements were just being flashed on the screen as they slid into their seats. The picture was not a particularly absorbing one, being an ex-aggerated portrayal of New York society life, and after the first few minutes, Nancy Drew's attention began to wander. At first she amused herself by studying the odd types of persons near her, but presently she began to think of Martha Frank and the queer way she had con-ducted herself in the old junk shop.

''I wonder what the quarrel was about?'' she

reflected. "It's strange she would have dealings with such a man."

Try as she would, Nancy could not forget the incident. She was still turning the matter over in her mind when the lights were flashed on in the theater. Alice, George and Bess promptly arose to depart.

"What?" Nancy demanded in surprise. "Is the picture over already?"

"I don't believe you saw a third of it," Bess accused her.

"Don't feel badly if you didn't," George cut in. "You didn't miss anything."

The girls filed out of the theater and made their way to the car where they found Mrs. Rawley waiting for them. Very soon Mr. Miller, who had also attended the show, put in his appearance and announced that he was ready to start for Shadow Ranch.

"Oh, Mr. Miller, do you know who owns that old junk shop on the main street not far from the theater?" Nancy inquired casually, as the foreman prepared to start the car.

"I reckon you mean Zany Shaw's place."

"What does the man look like? Is he short and sort of dried-up in appearance?"

"Yup, that's Zany all right. Sharp little eyes and a bald head as shiny as a new dollar!" The foreman bestowed a curious glance upon

Nancy. "Hope you gals ain't figgerin' on taking up with old Zany!"

"That relic!" George gave a contemptuous sniff.

"We saw Zany talking with Martha Frank," Nancy explained. "They both were quite angry."

"Did you say Martha Frank?"

Nancy nodded.

"Humph! I didn't know Martha could say enough words to quarrel with. Now I wonder what dealings she's had with old Zany?"

"We didn't hear much of the conversation," Nancy told him. "Only enough to know that he was threatening her about something. Perhaps with eviction."

" 'Twouldn't be that. Zany couldn't drive her off."

"What do you know of this man, anyway?"

"Nothin' good. Wouldn't surprise me if he'd escaped from some jail."

"How long has he been in Mougarstown?"

"Oh, about six years, maybe more for all I know. Never heard where he came from. Guess no one else ever did either. Close-mouthed, Zany is."

"He makes an honest living at the junk business?"

"Well, he makes a good livin'. I wouldn't swear as to the honest part. Folks haven't got much time for him around here. He's no account."

"What in particular have they against him?"

"Well, he's an old skinflint for one thing. He's never done anything that folks could hang on to him, but they've suspected enough. I wouldn't trust the old cod as far as I could see him."

"I do believe Nancy is trying to dig up another mystery," Bess declared, stifling a sleepy yawn.

"I was just asking a few questions," Nancy defended herself. "That doesn't mean anything."

"It does when you ask them in that particular intent way of yours," Bess insisted, with another yawn. "Oh, dear, what makes me so sleepy? It isn't nine-thirty yet."

"Time we were all back at the ranch," Mrs. Rawley declared, ending the discussion. "I believe this air has made me drowsy too."

During the trip back to Shadow Ranch nothing more was said about Zany Shaw or Martha Frank, but as far as Nancy Drew was concerned the subject was not closed. What she had learned, only served to whet her interest. Was it not possible, she asked herself, that she had accidently stumbled upon a mystery?

CHAPTER IX

A Picnic

"Girls, what do you say to a picnic in the mountains?"

George Fayne made the suggestion as she came out of the ranch house, her heavy riding boots clumping loudly on the veranda.

"Suits me," Nancy Drew declared, dropping her book. "If we go only a short way we shan't need a guide."

"If you girls go alone, I must insist that you take a revolver," Mrs. Rawley said, glancing up from the magazine she was reading. "Mr. Miller tells me that 'there's b'ar in them mountains.' "

"Oh, a bear wouldn't have a ghost of a show if he met four young huskies like us," George laughed. "However, we'll do as you suggest. Nancy can tote the gun because she's the only one that could hit the broad side of a barn."

"It would have to be a big barn," Nancy informed her. She turned to Bess, who was comfortably curled up in the hammock, and

76

ruthlessly dragged her to her feet. "Come on, don't be so lazy!"

"Must we go horseback?" Bess asked, with a martyred sigh. She glanced anxiously up at the sky.

"Oh, there's no danger of a storm," George told her. "There isn't a cloud in the sky. You'll enjoy the outing once you get started."

"Perhaps," Bess muttered, but she went inside to change to her riding costume.

Alice followed her, while Nancy and George, who were already dressed for the outing, hurried to the kitchen to prepare the luncheon. By the time Bess and Alice were ready they had packed the knapsacks and had brought the ponies to the fence.

"Don't forget the gun," Mrs. Rawley reminded the girls as they were about to start.

Nancy ran into the house, returning in a minute with a revolver in a holster at her belt.

"I feel like a walking arsenal," she laughed, as she swung into the saddle.

The girls started off at a brisk trot and were soon out of sight from the ranch house. Reaching the mountain, they selected a trail which one of the cowboys had recommended, but were forced to slow their ponies to a walk as it was very steep. For perhaps an hour they climbed steadily and then halted for a brief rest as Bess and Alice were beginning to tire. After a time they continued until they came to a crystal-clear stream which provided an excellent site for the picnic meal.

"Let's stop here," Bess suggested. "We've gone far enough."

The others were well satisfied with the location, so halted their ponies. Tying them to a tree, they spread out their luncheon a short distance away and were not surprised to find that they had developed hearty appetites.

"I'm getting fatter every day of my life," Bess complained as she munched a sandwich. "This is my third."

"Fifth you mean," George corrected her brutally.

After the luncheon things had been cleared away, the girls stretched themselves on the grass.

"I suppose we should be starting for home," Nancy observed.

"Oh, let's rest first," George said. "I feel like having a siesta."

Pillowing her head upon her arms, she promptly closed her eyes. The others followed her example. Nancy had no intention of permitting herself to fall asleep, but before she knew it she had dozed off.

Presently she awoke with a start and sat up. What had awakened her? She glanced toward

George and saw that she too had opened her eyes.

"What was that?" she whispered to George.

Even as she spoke there was a great commotion in the thicket and one of the ponies gave a snort of fright. Instantly, Nancy Drew was on her feet. By this time Bess and Alice were aroused and they too were frightened.

"Oh, what can it be?" Alice whispered.

Cautiously, the four girls moved forward, Nancy Drew in the lead with her revolver held ready for instant use. They paused and huddled together as though for mutual protection when they heard another rustling in the bushes not far from where the ponies were tied.

"Oh, let's not go any nearer," Alice begged.

Just at that moment Bess gave a little scream and pointed toward the thicket.

"I saw a great big cat there in the bushes!"

Nancy did not respond, for the ponies, evidently excited at the approach of the wild animal, began to plunge and rear, pulling at their bridles.

"Whoa! Whoa!" Nancy called, but her efforts were wasted.

Even as she ran forward, a cat-like animal flashed out from the thicket. It was probable that the girls had not securely tied their ponies, for they broke away from the restraining tree branch and charged down the trail.

"Whoa!" George shouted frantically. "Whoa! Stop! Come back here!"

She started to run after them, but saw at once that it was useless, and halted. Bess and Alice, who had been too frightened to try to head off the ponies, clutched each other in a frenzy of terror.

"Oh!" Bess suddenly cried. "That cat! There it is!"

At the same moment Nancy caught a glimpse of the prowling lynx. Taking aim, she fired.

The bullet struck the animal in the shoulder. It snarled and turned, ready to spring.

Her heart in her throat, for she realized that she must not fail, Nancy fired once more.

As the bullet found its mark, there was a terrible crashing and smashing in the underbrush, and then all was quiet.

"I must have got him," Nancy cried excitedly.

"Let's look," George suggested courageously, but Bess held her back.

"Don't you go near there. That big cat might not be dead."

"It's a lynx," Nancy corrected.

"Well, I don't care what it is, I don't want to see it. George, don't you dare go near!"

"All right," George agreed, for in spite of

her courageous words she was not particularly
eager to step into the thicket. "Still, I think
we might take it home and have it stuffed."

"Home!" Nancy exclaimed. "Do you girls
realize that we're at least seven or eight miles
from the ranch?"

"And our ponies gone!" Alice murmured.

"Can't we get them?" Bess demanded anxiously.

"Get them?" George snorted. "They're
probably a mile from here already!"

"But surely they'll go back to the ranch,"
Bess protested. "In that case, Aunt Nell will
know something is wrong and send someone
after us."

"That's our only hope," Alice observed.

"Then we can just sit down here on the grass
and if that old lynx doesn't bother us any more,
take it easy until the rescue party arrives,"
George announced.

"But what if the ponies don't happen to go
back to the ranch?" Nancy asked quietly. "In
that case—" her voice trailed off.

"In that case," George finished with a show
of optimism, "We'll just have to walk home."

"Walk eight miles?" Bess gasped. "I never
walked that far in my life."

"Oh, well, it's likely a party from the ranch
will meet us on the trail," Nancy declared.
"However, I think it will be wisest for us to

start off at once.'' She glanced at her wrist watch and frowned slightly. ''It won't be many hours until it will get dark.''

''I don't want to stay here, anyway,'' Bess said with an uneasy glance in the direction of the thicket.

''All right, let's go,'' George agreed. ''But first I want to have a look and see if Nancy really got that old lynx.''

''George!'' her cousin screamed.

Ignoring Bess, George pulled the bushes apart. Nancy, although she was certain that her shot had finished the animal, came close to the girl's side, at the same time putting two new cartridges into the revolver.

''You got him all right,'' George observed with satisfaction. ''What a wicked old fellow too! Come on girls, and have a look!''

''Never!'' Bess announced firmly.

Nor could George persuade Alice to venture near.

''Come on, George,'' Nancy urged. ''We really must get started.''

Gloomily, the four girls set off down the trail. Not until they were a safe distance from the thicket did Bess relax.

''Cheer up, girls!'' George encouraged the others as they trudged along. ''Eight miles isn't so far.''

''Only a little more than forty two thousand

feet," Bess grumbled. "By the time I've taken that many steps I'll be a complete wreck."

Alice did not speak as the girls walked along, and several times Nancy glanced toward her. She knew that the girl was not as strong as the others and already she looked tired and wan. Would she become exhausted before they reached the ranch?

Though Nancy had not communicated her fears to the others, she had little hope that a searching party would set out after them for several hours. Before that time it would be dark on the mountain. Involuntarily, her hand touched the holster at her belt. How thankful she was that Mrs. Rawley had insisted she carry the revolver. The indications were that before the night was over she would again have need of it.

CHAPTER X

A Long Tramp Home

"Oh, dear, I'm about ready to drop! How far do you suppose we are from the ranch now?"

Bess Marvin asked the question as with a weary sigh she sank down upon a flat stone to rest. For some time the girls had trudged bravely down the steep mountain trail, but with fatigue had come discouragement, and Bess had been the first to falter.

"I'm afraid we have at least four miles yet before us," Nancy told her as she too sat down. "It begins to look as though that searching party isn't coming after us."

"Well, I guess we deserved what we got," George admitted, as she unlaced one of her boots. "We should have tied our ponies more securely."

"They'll think we're the worst sort of tenderfeet at the ranch," Nancy observed gloomily.

"They won't think that about you when we tell how you shot that big lynx," Alice said.

84

"I don't think we'll ever get to the ranch to tell anybody about anything," Bess announced pessimistically. "What's the matter, George? Feet hurt you?"

By this time George had removed her boot and was gingerly examining a blister on her heel.

"Oh, I'll manage to hobble along," she returned with a show of indifference. "It's Alice here who is about ready to give up the ghost."

"I can still go some way farther," Alice insisted.

Nancy, who had been gazing anxiously toward the horizon, now arose.

"Girls, I don't want to alarm you, but I think we should be starting along. The sun is getting low and I'm afraid it won't be long until it will be dark."

"Oh!" Bess hastily got up, casting a frightened glance toward the bushes. "I'll die of fright if we're stranded on this mountain after dark. Wild animals will be prowling about and it will be dreadful!"

"It won't be pleasant, that's certain," Nancy said grimly.

George quickly laced up her boot and announced that she was ready to go on. Silently the girls trudged down the trail, at a more rapid pace than before, for the fear of being caught on the mountain after dark was upon them all. Yet Nancy, who was bringing up the rear, observed that George was limping and she knew what that meant. They would soon be forced to slacken their speed.

However, it was not George but Alice who brought the party to a halt. She had become so tired that she could not go on without a brief rest. By the time the girls took to the trail again the sun had vanished below the horizon line. Very shortly darkness descended upon the mountain.

"Cheer up, girls," Nancy said as cheerfully as she could. "We must be near Martha Frank's cottage."

The words were scarcely out of her mouth when George, who was in the lead, gave a little scream.

"Oh, my ankle! I've turned it!"

With a moan of pain George sank to the ground, nursing the injured member. The others gathered about her sympathetically.

"Of all the stupid things to do!" George muttered, trying not to let on how severe the pain was.

"Let me see it," Nancy directed. She stooped down and ran a gentle hand over the injured ankle. "It's swelling. I'll wrap it up with a handkerchief but I'm afraid that's the

best we can do until we get to the ranch. Do
you think you can walk?"

"Of course I can."

George got to her feet, but the first step
caused her to cringe with pain.

"It just about kills you, doesn't it?" Nancy
asked.

George shook her head stubbornly.

"I can walk."

However, before she had taken a dozen steps,
the others were convinced that she was suffer-
ing severe pain and insisted that she lean upon
someone for support. In spite of her protest,
they took turns helping her along.

They had not progressed far down the path
when Nancy called a halt. There was a little
tremor to her voice as she spoke.

"Girls, I hate to say it, but I wonder if we're
still on the trail. I'm sure we never came
this way."

"I was thinking the same thing," Alice declared, "but I was afraid to let myself believe it."

"We must have taken the wrong turn back
there where George turned her ankle," Nancy
decided. "There's nothing we can do but go
back."

Fortunately, the girls had not come a great
distance and soon reached the turn in the trail.

As Nancy had surmised, they found that they had taken a path which had branched off to the right when they should have taken the one to the left.

"We'll soon reach Martha's cabin now," Nancy declared. "It can't be a quarter of a mile."

Doggedly, they plodded on, encouraged to think that they were coming to the end of the trail. Presently, Nancy caught a glimpse of a light shining through the trees.

"That must be the cottage," she told the others eagerly.

"What if Martha won't let us in?" Alice asked wearily.

"I don't believe she'd be heartless enough to turn us away," Nancy responded. "If she tries to—well, we'll decide that when the time comes."

When she rapped sharply on the cabin door some ten minutes later, Nancy scarcely knew what sort of reception to expect. She was not at all surprised when Martha Frank opened the door and stared at the girls hostilely as though questioning their right to come near her cottage. Nancy explained what had happened.

"Please, we'd like to come in and rest for a few minutes," she begged.

Martha Frank scowled darkly and the girls thought that she was about to refuse, but instead she muttered something under her breath and stepped aside for them to enter. Once inside, Nancy and her friends sank wearily down into the nearest chairs and for the time being did not mind the old woman's disinclination to conversation.

"I wonder if I could have a drink of water?" Nancy asked, after several minutes had elapsed. "And we'd like to have a little heated so that we can bathe my friend's ankle."

Martha Frank did not respond, but took a bucket from the table and left the cabin, apparently to get water from a well or a spring.

"Sociable as ever," George commented dryly.

"As soon as we're rested let's get away from here," Alice pleaded. "There's something about this place that gives me the creeps."

At that moment Nancy Drew held up her hand for silence, and the others, gazing at her in surprise, saw that her eyes were riveted upon the bedroom door. Following her glance they saw two eyes peeping through a crack at them.

"It must be that child they call Lucy," Bess whispered. "I wonder if she heard what we said?"

"It doesn't matter," Nancy returned in a low voice.

She got up and walked toward the bedroom door.

"Lucy, why don't you come out and talk with us? We won't hurt you."

The door opened a trifle wider, but it took considerable coaxing before Lucy was persuaded to venture forth. She kept casting frightened glances toward the door as though expecting Martha Frank to return at any minute.

Nancy too glanced anxiously toward the door, for she hoped that the woman would not return until she had had an opportunity to draw Lucy into conversation. There were a great many questions which she wished to ask, and well she knew that the return of Martha would put an end to any such plan.

"Don't be afraid, Lucy," she repeated gently. "We won't hurt you."

"I'm not afraid of you," the child returned soberly. "It's *her* I'm scared of. She beats me when I talk with folks."

Before Nancy could ask questions, heavy footsteps were heard on the path.

"She's coming," Lucy whispered fearfully. "If she catches me out here she'll half kill me after you go!"

With that, the child shot across the room to the bedroom, softly closing the door behind her.

CHAPTER XI

A Visitor

Scarcely had Lucy Brown disappeared into the bedroom when Martha Frank came into the kitchen with the bucket of water. She glanced sharply about, and for an instant Nancy thought that she must have seen the child. However, the woman appeared to be satisfied, for she turned to put a teakettle of water on the stove.

As soon as the water was warm Nancy carefully bathed George's swollen ankle and wrapped it with a clean rag which Martha grudgingly provided. Now that the girls were a trifle rested, she thought it best that they continue to the ranch before Mrs. Rawley became alarmed for their safety, yet she was unwilling to depart until she had learned more about Lucy. If it were true that Martha mistreated her, she considered it her duty to inform the authorities and have them transfer the child to a better home. She decided to draw the old woman into conversation if possible.

"I thought perhaps I would get to see your

little girl again," she began pleasantly. "She is your child, isn't she?"

The woman stared at her hard and then, when Nancy had made up her mind that she would not answer, said:

"What's it to you?"

"Why, nothing at all," Nancy returned with her most disarming smile. "I was merely curious."

"Curiosity's got lots of folks into trouble, young lady."

With that, Martha turned her back and began to busy herself at the stove.

"Let's go," George whispered. "My ankle doesn't hurt as much as it did."

Nancy was convinced that she would learn nothing from Martha Frank, and, as the others were eager to depart, took leave of the cottage. Once outside they all breathed more freely.

"What possesses that woman?" Bess demanded when they were some distance away. "I was afraid if we stayed there any longer she would use her shotgun on us."

"She's an old crab," George declared. "I thought at first she must be dumb, but I guess she can use her tongue when she wants to. Imagine telling Nancy to mind her own business!"

"I feel sorry for that child," Nancy said slowly. "She's not a bit like Martha."

"Girls!" Alice exclaimed suddenly. "Look down the trail! I do believe they've sent a party out from the ranch to look for us!"

"Praises be!" George ejaculated. "It's Mr. Miller and Jim True and they're leading our horses!"

Eagerly the girls hailed the two approaching riders and received answering shouts.

"I'm not going to take another step," Alice murmured. "Let them come and get us."

"I wish they had brought a stretcher," Nancy sighed wearily. "I'd enjoy being carried back to the ranch in state."

As the two men rode up, the girls forgot their resolution to remain where they were, and rushed out to greet them. Quickly, they poured out their tale of woe and were grateful that neither Mr. Miller nor Jim True smiled when they mentioned the lynx.

"We'd best get back to Shadow Ranch as quickly as we can," the foreman advised. "Mrs. Rawley is worryin' her head off. The ponies came home and right off we knew something had happened to you gals."

"I don't think I'll ever be able to walk again," Bess sighed.

Yet, for all her good-natured complaining, Bess Marvin had stood the ordeal better than either Alice or George. The former was so nearly exhausted that when she was lifted from the saddle at Shadow Ranch, she would have fallen had not Nancy caught her by the arm.

"You girls go straight to bed just the minute you have had something warm to eat," Mrs. Rawley told them anxiously. "What would your mothers say to me if they thought I hadn't taken proper care of you?"

"We're all right, Aunt Nell," George told her. "Thanks to you, we had the revolver along, and after this we'll always take it."

"After this?" Mrs. Rawley echoed weakly.

George Miller chuckled softly.

"They'll learn! From now on they'll take pains to tie their ponies better. They ain't the first that's walked home from the mountains."

With this consolation ringing in their ears, the girls ate their supper and tumbled into bed. The next morning they slept late and George did not put in her appearance until luncheon time. The others noticed at once that she was still limping.

"Oh, I suppose I'll be on the shelf for a day or so," she admitted when they questioned her concerning her swollen ankle.

"We've all decided to make it a quiet day," Nancy told her. "Mrs. Rawley says we're to sit around and do nothing but read, talk and rest."

"I'm sure that plan meets my whole-hearted approval," Bess murmured.

After luncheon, the girls settled themselves on the veranda, but if they had anticipated a dull afternoon it was not to be. Scarcely had they picked up magazines when Jim True appeared at the corral with a bronco which he was endeavoring to break. At once three girls rushed to the fence to see the fun, George limping in the rear. It was while they were perched on the top rail that Nancy chanced to look toward the road.

"Why, someone is coming!" she cried.

The others turned to look and were surprised to see a car driving into the lane which led to Shadow Ranch. As visitors were rare indeed, bronco breaking immediately lost its interest.

"I wonder who it is?" George asked. "Probably someone to see Mrs. Rawley about buying the ranch."

"Girls, it's our old friend, Mr. Rogers!" Nancy announced, as the car drew nearer.

"What's he coming here for?" Bess asked suspiciously.

"Why, to see us, of course," Nancy told her. "Don't you remember? Mrs. Rawley invited him out here."

"Yes, but she never thought he would come."

"Well, I'm glad he did."

As she spoke, Nancy hurried forward to greet the newcomer and the others followed. Mrs. Rawley had noted the approach of the automobile from the veranda and she too left her chair to welcome Ross Rogers.

"I am so glad you came," she told him graciously. "Won't you sit on the veranda with us? I think Mrs. Miller is just making lemonade, and a cool drink should prove refreshing after your trip."

"Thank you," the man responded with an embarrassed smile.

He followed Mrs. Rawley and the girls to the ranch house and there seemed more at ease. He did not talk a great deal but sipped his lemonade with evident enjoyment and took a keen interest in everything that was said. It seemed to Nancy, who had been watching him, that he appeared tired and worn out as though from a long sickness. It was upon the tip of her tongue to ask him if he had been ill when she caught herself, thinking that since he had not brought up the subject such a question might appear inquisitive.

Presently, conversation began to lag and Mrs. Rawley, hoping to fill an awkward gap, remarked:

"I wonder if by any chance we could be distantly related? You know, my maiden name was Rogers."

The man stared at her for an instant, and a deep flush crept over his face.

"No, no," he muttered nervously. "Every-

one calls me Rogers, but my name is really
Roger."

"Roger?"

The man avoided Mrs. Rawley's steady gaze.

"Yes, I'm sure it's Roger."

There was an awkward silence and then Mrs.
Rawley with her usual tact, stepped into the
breach.

"In that case, we couldn't be related. Nancy,
would you mind asking Mrs. Miller for another
pitcher of lemonade?"

Nancy arose, but before she could go to the
kitchen, Ross Rogers also got up and announced
that he must be leaving.

"But you haven't been here a half hour,"
Mrs. Rawley protested.

"I shouldn't have closed the store this long,
I'm afraid," he murmured uncomfortably. "I
really must be going."

"Then of course we won't try to detain
you any longer."

Hastily saying good-bye, Mr. Rogers hurried
down the path to his car. The girls watched
him until he had disappeared beyond the bend
in the road.

"Well, that man is stupid!" George broke
out. "Imagine not knowing your own name!"

"There's something wrong with him," Bess
insisted.

Mrs. Rawley frowned thoughtfully and said

nothing, but she wondered, too, about him.

"Don't be too hard on the poor man," Nancy chided. "He didn't impress me as being stupid. Of course, he didn't seem to be sure of his name—but perhaps there's a reason."

"I think he was just shy and embarrassed," Alice added kindly. "He's awfully nice."

"Yes, I like him too," Bess admitted grudgingly. "But I can't help but notice that he acted suspiciously."

"It was odd that he hurried off the way he did," Nancy remarked, more to herself than for the benefit of the others.

"Well, I don't think we'll need to worry about him any more," Mrs. Rawley said quietly. "Unless I am mistaken, he'll not come here again."

"I'm sure I've seen him some place before that day I met him on the train," Nancy declared, speaking slowly. "If only I could recall——"

Suddenly, she sprang up from the steps where she was sitting and whirled upon the others.

"Girls, I have it! It came back to me all at once! George, don't you remember him?"

"Can't say that I do."

"Why, he was a teller in the River Heights First National Bank. As I recall, he worked there about six months and then drifted away."

"I do remember him now!" George declared.

"Wasn't he the one that got a job because he rescued the bank president's daughter from being run over by a reckless automobile driver?"

Nancy nodded, her eyes alight with excitement.

"There was nothing stupid about him when he worked in the bank, either!"

"Why did he leave?" Mrs. Rawley questioned. "I hope he didn't get into trouble."

"Oh, no, he just disappeared without any apparent reason. No one ever heard of him again."

"Until we met him out here," Alice supplied.

"It certainly is a baffling case," Nancy said, a tense quality creeping into her voice. "He knew we came from River Heights and he never let on that he had ever heard of the place! Now I wonder——"

But what it was that had occurred to her she did not say.

CHAPTER XII

An Interlude

Mrs. Rawley was correct in her prediction concerning Ross Rogers—or Roger. In the days that followed he did not again visit Shadow Ranch.

Nancy Drew was secretly disappointed for she had looked forward to talking with the man again. She told herself that before she left the West she would call upon him at his book and stationery shop in Mougarstown and ask him pointblank if he had ever lived in River Heights.

"There's something queer about the whole affair," she told herself more than once. "I believe he must have had a very particular reason for leaving town the way he did, and I'd like to know what it was. Perhaps he is in trouble and needs help."

The days sped along and the girls were having such good times that they did not have occasion to go to Mougarstown. Not in the least daunted by their early misadventures, they rode horseback and roamed the mountain

trails, gained weight, and developed smooth
coats of tan. As they became more familiar
with the various mountain paths they ventured
farther and farther from the ranch.

"You'll get lost yet," Mrs. Rawley told them.
"Don't forget you've already had two unpleasant adventures."

"Two?" Alice laughed. "I think we've had
a dozen at least! Did Nancy tell you about
that rattler she shot yesterday?"

Mrs. Rawley shuddered.

"No, she didn't tell me! Gracious! What
will happen to you girls next?"

"I hope we don't have any more encounters
with bears, anyway!" Bess put in. "I never
have forgiven that one that got into our lunch
basket."

Mrs. Rawley sighed.

"It's a wonder it didn't get you instead.
I'll not breathe easy again until I take you girls
safely back to the city."

"Poor Aunt Nell!" George sympathized.
"You may feel better to know that we're going
only a short way into the mountains to-day.
We've decided to try a little fishing."

In a very short time the four girls had lost
all of their former timidity and no longer required a guide when they ventured into the
mountains in quest of adventure. To be sure,
Bess and Alice had not taken whole-heartedly

to the wild life; when snakes or foxes were encountered they were willing that Nancy and George should take the initiative.

Frequently the girls rode horseback into the mountains, but when their excursions were not long ones they preferred to hike.

On this particular day they planned to fish for trout in a stream which George Miller had assured them would provide excellent sport. Early in the afternoon they started out, but either the foreman's information was incorrect or the girls were not sufficiently skilled to cope with the wary trout, for after an hour's casting, they did not have a fish in their basket.

"Bess makes too big a splash when she drops her fly on the water," George complained. "She might just as well throw a rock and be done with it!"

"I don't see that you're doing so much better yourself," Bess retorted hotly. "You have your line all tangled up in the bushes this minute."

"It certainly wasn't my fault the tree was in the way."

"Sh!" Nancy warned. "The fish will hear you, and we won't catch a one!"

"They're probably down at the bottom of the pool having a good laugh anyway," George returned.

"I wouldn't put it past them," Nancy

agreed. "They say trout are remarkably intelligent fish. They have a keen sense of sight as well as hearing."

"I suppose that being the case we should have sneaked up on them," Alice commented.

Nancy made a neat cast into the center of the pool and then reeled in with a discouraged sigh.

"I suspect we're using the wrong kind of bait. Now if I only had a big fat worm——"

"Nancy Drew, I wouldn't have come along if you hadn't promised me you wouldn't use those horrid, crawly things," Bess reminded her friend sternly.

"I haven't any to use. As far as I'm concerned I'm ready to call it a day."

The others were more than willing to start for Shadow Ranch, for although they had enjoyed the outing, it had been hard work to tramp up and down the stream searching for likely pools. Gathering together their fishing tackle, they set off for home.

"Well, I guess we'll get back one time at least without an adventure," Alice remarked as they hiked along.

"Without any fish, too," George added.

The girls had continued perhaps a hundred yards down the trail when Bess abruptly halted and glanced back.

"What's the matter?" George demanded.

"I—I thought I heard a rustling in the bushes behind us! Oh, George, I——"

"Oh, there you go again! Bess, you're always hearing things!"

"I did hear something. I know I did."

"Bess is right," Nancy said quietly. "I heard a rustling noise myself, but it's probably only a small animal. Probably a rabbit."

"Whatever it was, it made too much noise for that," Bess protested earnestly.

"You might go and peek in the bushes," George suggested mischievously to her cousin.

"There's no use inviting trouble," Nancy observed soberly. "It's probably nothing to cause alarm, but we had best be prepared. George, if you'll hand over the revolver, I'll bring up the rear."

George looked guilty.

"Don't tell me you didn't bring it!" Nancy cried. "You said you'd get it out of the bureau drawer for me."

"I know I did, but I forgot all about it. I went into the house to get it and then Aunt Nell called me and I never thought of it again."

Nancy's face became grave, but she did not criticize her friend for her carelessness.

"This is a poor time to be without it, but perhaps we can get along."

Hastily, the four went on down the path, Nancy bringing up the rear.

They had not gone far until the rustling noise was again heard, and this time it seemed closer.

"Oh, I know there's a wild animal following us!" Bess breathed fearfully.

"Don't stop to think about it!" Nancy commanded sharply as the girl would have paused. "Let's get to the clearing as fast as we can!"

Still came the stealthy pad, pad to their right and a little behind them. The girls slowed their pace. Still the pad, pad without approaching nearer but without dropping behind. The girls hurried on again. Pad, pad came the sound, keeping pace with the frightened girls.

"Why not run?" Alice suggested nervously.

"No, I think we had better walk as fast as we can instead. If we start to run it might bring on an attack."

Though the girls did not catch a glimpse of the beast which was stalking them, they continued to hear the soft pad, pad of footsteps behind them, and at every moment their terror increased. If only they could reach the clearing!

CHAPTER XIII

Stalked by a Cougar

Fearfully, Nancy and her friends hastened down the path toward the clearing which they could see only a short distance ahead. Behind them came the steady pad of their unseen enemy. Now they could hear the footsteps drawing nearer until it seemed that the animal must surely pounce out upon them.

"Keep a steady nerve," Nancy advised the others. "We'll make it all right."

As she spoke, she again heard a rustling, crashing of the bushes and looked quickly over her shoulder. A chill passed over her as she caught a brief glimpse of a large animal in the path not fifty yards behind her. It was a cougar!

Bess too, had seen the animal, and with a little scream of terror, raced toward the clearing. Of one accord, the others broke into a run.

Breathless, they reached the clearing, but did not halt there or glance back. At breakneck speed they sought to put as great a distance between themselves and the cougar as possible. Not until they caught sight of a group of cowboys riding toward them did they dare to pause. They called to the men and were relieved to receive answering shouts.

"A narrow escape!" Nancy murmured.

Quickly, she told the cowboys, who came from the Bar X Ranch, of the cougar which was stalking them.

"Don't worry," they assured her. "We'll get him all right! A cougar hasn't ventured this close to a ranch for years."

After asking where the animal was last seen, the riders galloped away and were swallowed up by the forest.

"Aunt Nell will have nervous prostration when she learns about this," George declared, as the girls continued toward the ranch. "It does seem as though we were destined for adventure and breath-taking escapes."

"I suppose we'll have to tell her," Bess admitted. "The story's certain to get around."

"Oh, well, I guess she's getting hardened to our escapades by this time," Nancy laughed. "As long as we came out of it all right, there's no harm done."

Reaching the ranch house, the girls found that there was no need to trouble Mrs. Rawley with an account of their adventure, for she had gone to Mougarstown to attend to some business concerning the sale of the ranch. She had left a note saying that she would not return until late in the evening and suggested that the girls drive to Mougarstown to attend a dance, returning with her.

"What a grand idea!" Nancy declared. "I've been wanting to get to town for a week."

"I hope we meet some nice men," Bess put in.

"So do I, for your sake," George teased. "Your trip will be a failure if you don't capture the heart of at least one handsome cowbay."

As soon as they had finished supper, the girls dressed in their best party frocks, and with Mr. Miller as driver, started off in the old car.

"Mrs. Rawley left word that she would call for us at the dance," Nancy remarked as they drove along. "My, did you ever see so many automobiles in town? Everyone in the country must be going to the dance."

Mr. Miller let the girls out in front of a brightly lighted hall. They entered somewhat uncertainly, but as they saw a number of familiar faces they felt more at ease. One of the cowboys from the Bar X Ranch, whom the girls had met during the round-up, came to claim Nancy for the first dance.

"I heard all about your mountain lion," he

told her as the music struck up and they glided off together. "The boys got it all right—an ugly specimen."

After the dance ended, he brought up several friends and introduced them to Nancy and the others. Bess was quite taken with a young lawyer, David Glaston, and as the feeling was mutual, there were no dull moments for her that evening. George and Alice were never without partners, while Nancy was in so much demand that she was forced to refuse dances. The girls had a splendid time, but for some reason Nancy did not appear as carefree as the others.

"What's the matter?" George asked her when they had a moment alone. "Aren't you having a good time?"

"Of course I am, George. What makes you think I'm not?"

"Oh, you look so thoughtful and you keep glancing around. Aunt Nell will get here soon enough."

"I'm in no hurry to leave."

At this moment Doctor Cole came up to claim Nancy for the next dance. He was one of the young men she had met during the evening, and she found him unusually interesting. But as they danced away together, it was all she could do to keep her mind on what he was saying.

The truth was that Nancy had hoped to see Ross Rogers at the dance, and in this she had been disappointed. Involuntarily, her eyes had searched the crowd for a glimpse of him. Even now, as she danced with Doctor Cole, her eyes wandered over the group of bystanders.

Then she saw him. He was standing at one corner of the room looking across toward Alice Regor who was chatting with one of the cowboys from the Bar X. Nancy was struck by the melancholy expression upon his face.

"Why doesn't he go over and speak to the girls?" she asked herself.

As she whirled about the floor she managed to keep an eye upon him, and when the music ceased it was not entirely chance that brought Nancy and Doctor Cole to where the man was standing. She introduced Ross Rogers, whom, however, Doctor Cole already knew, and after the three had chatted pleasantly for a few minutes, the doctor left them together.

Nancy felt that her opportunity had arrived. Skillfully leading up to the subject, she remarked casually:

"Do you know, you remind me of someone I once knew in River Heights."

Ross Rogers stared at her an instant and then lowered his eyes.

"That's strange," he murmured after a long moment of silence.

Nancy waited but he said nothing more. As the music started again, he glanced anxiously toward the door. His hands were trembling.

"I must be getting back," he mumbled, avoiding Nancy's eyes.

With that, he turned and walked swiftly away.

CHAPTER XIV

A Visit to the Cottage

"Well, of all things!" Nancy murmured, as Ross Rogers walked hurriedly away. "What can be the matter with that man? Is he afraid I'll find out something about him?"

She was not permitted to meditate long on the strange actions of her new friend, for just then Doctor Cole came over to claim the next dance. However, before the music started, Alice approached to tell Nancy that Mrs. Rawley had arrived and was ready to start for the ranch.

With their escorts, the girls crossed the room to where she was standing, and introductions were quickly accomplished. After chatting for a few minutes, Mrs. Rawley cordially invited the young men to call at the ranch, an invitation which they promptly accepted. After saying good-bye, the girls left the hall.

"I guess that doctor has quite a case on Nancy," Bess teased as they drove home. "I know he'll not forget Aunt Nell's invitation."

"How about that lawyer friend of yours?"

Nancy countered. "What was it he whispered to you just as we left? You don't dare tell!"

Bess blushed furiously.

"Oh, it wasn't anything at all. He just said he thought it would be a good idea if we got up a riding party for some moonlight night."

"Ha!" Nancy exclaimed. "A moonlight night! That sounds as though it's getting serious."

"It won't be after he sees how badly I ride."

"Say, Nancy," George broke in, "wasn't that Ross Rogers you were talking with?"

Nancy nodded.

"Did he have any more to say than usual?"

"Less, if anything."

Nancy said no more, for she had decided not to relate what had happened. She felt that to do so would only prejudice the girls against the man. In her own mind she was convinced that he had intended no slight, but the others might not interpret his action so kindly.

"I'm going to forget all about him," she told herself. "It's obvious he doesn't care to have his past known, and I have no right to go prying into his affairs."

In the next few days Nancy did succeed in forgetting Ross Rogers, for another matter came up which captured her attention. Since the time that she had managed to have a few words with Lucy Brown, Nancy had been eager to return to the cottage of Martha Frank, but an opportunity had not presented itself. It was not until a week after the night of the dance that circumstance again brought her to the old cabin.

The girls had been riding in the mountains, as was now their daily custom, when Nancy observed that the sky was overcast. At once they started for the ranch, but it was evident that it would rain before they could reach home.

"Let's stop at the cottage," Nancy suggested. "The rain can't last very long."

"I think I'd almost as soon get wet as have that iceberg stare at me the way she does," George declared.

"I'd like to talk with that child again," Nancy said. "You girls ride on to the ranch without me."

"If you stop, so do we!" Alice insisted firmly.

The others were of the same mind, so they rode up and tied their horses to a tree not far from the cottage.

"It looks to me as though there's no one at home," Bess observed as they approached. "The door is open and Martha Frank usually has it closed so tight you couldn't find a crack to peep through."

"No, there's someone inside," Nancy said,

speaking quietly. "I can hear a noise in the bedroom."

She entered the cottage, the others following rather timidly.

"What if it's Martha?" Bess breathed fearfully. "She'll take her shotgun to us, that's what she'll do!"

Without replying, Nancy crossed over to the bedroom and opened the door. As she had guessed, it was Lucy Brown who occupied the room.

"Oh!"

With an exclamation of surprise and alarm, Lucy wheeled about as the door swung on its hinges. Seeing Nancy and her friends, the child jerked up a pile of garments from the floor beside her, crammed them into a trunk, and slammed down the lid.

"Don't be frightened," Nancy said gently.

"Did *she* see you come in?" Lucy demanded sharply, with another anxious glance toward the old trunk.

"No, you have no cause to be alarmed on that score. Why is it you are so afraid of Martha Frank?"

"Oh, she beats me nearly ever time she comes back from town."

"Is that where your grandmother has gone to-day?"

Lucy nodded.

"She isn't my grandmother, though. I don't think she's any relation to me at all or she wouldn't treat me the way she does. She'll lam me good if she finds I've been in this trunk again."

"You were told not to open it?"

"Yes, but I did. I wanted to play with the doll."

"Doll?" Nancy inquired with interest. "Won't you show it to me?"

"I wouldn't dare. *She* might come!"

"I really must see the inside of that trunk," Nancy said, speaking more to herself than for the benefit of the child. "Its contents may answer a good many questions that have been troubling me."

She walked over to the trunk, and while Lucy watched with frightened eyes, lifted the lid. There before her was the doll Lucy had mentioned, but so handsomely was it dressed that Nancy's eyes opened wide in surprise. The trunk contained a number of small boxes as well as a pile of tiny garments which would have fit a child of three or four years.

"What a find!" Nancy exclaimed.

The others gathered about the trunk, even more excited than she.

"Does Martha ever let you play with this doll?" Nancy asked Lucy.

"No, she says I'll break it, but I don't think that's her real reason."

"Neither do I," Nancy murmured. Turning to the child again, she asked: "Do you know where this trunk came from?"

Again Lucy shook her head.

"It's been here ever since I can remember."

Eagerly, Nancy snatched up one of the tiny dresses from the pile and examined its fine material and real lace trimming.

"Where do you suppose Martha got dresses such as these?" she demanded of the others. "It begins to look suspicious to me!"

Upon sudden impulse she turned one of the dresses inside out and looked at the label.

"Goodman and Goodman, Philadelphia!" she read in amazement.

"Look here what I've found in this box!" George broke in. "Child's jewelry."

She displayed a tiny ring set with genuine pearls and a small necklace. Before Nancy could examine the find, Lucy emitted a little squeal of fright.

"Oh, someone is coming up the path! If I get caught——"

Nancy wheeled about and glanced out of the window. Less than a stone's throw away was Zany Shaw, the Mougarstown junk dealer, and he was heading straight for the cottage.

"Quick!" she commanded. "Get the things back into the trunk!"

Frantically, the girls replaced the articles they had removed and closed the lid. They retreated hastily to the other room, shutting the door behind them.

They were not an instant too soon. Scarcely had they reached the outside room when Zany Shaw came up to the door. He did not rap, but entered boldly. Seeing the girls, he stopped short and stared at them. Then an angry gleam came into his eyes.

"What are you doing here?" he demanded harshly. "Get out before I put you out!"

CHAPTER XV

NANCY DREW faced Zany Shaw fearlessly, and her eyes did not waver under his furious glare. Though Alice Regor and Bess Marvin had edged nearer the door, and George Fayne was plucking at her sleeve trying to draw her away, she had no intention of retreating. She knew that she had done nothing wrong, and for that reason refused to be frightened away from the cottage.

"What are you doing here?" Zany demanded again, taking a step toward her.

"What are you doing here yourself?" Nancy countered. "Tell me that!"

The old junk dealer hesitated, apparently taken aback at the question. He looked confused and muttered:

"I came to see Martha Frank."

"I saw you talking with her at Mougarstown," Nancy said pointedly, all the time watching the man shrewdly. "You were threatening her then. How do I know that you don't intend to harm her?"

Zany involuntarily took a step backward, and for an instant a frightened look was in his eyes. Then he smiled.

"You are mistaken," he insisted vehemently, beginning to gesticulate with his hands. "I have not seen Martha Frank in a good many months. I came to-day to collect a bill she owes me."

"At any rate, you have no right to order us out! We came here to get out of the storm, and we intend to stay."

Not for a moment did Nancy really believe that Zany had told his true reason for coming to the cottage, but wisely refrained from accusing the man of a deliberate falsehood. She had no desire to start trouble, but, on the other hand, had no intention of allowing him to force her away.

Evidently, Zany read the determination in Nancy's face, for his manner changed abruptly, and he began to offer profuse apologies.

"I thought you had broken into the cottage," he told her. "I am very sorry——"

"Do we look as though we would break into people's houses?" Nancy asked sharply.

"No, no," Zany assured her hastily. "It was my mistake—my mistake." He backed toward the door. "I will come back again when Martha Frank is here."

Walking hurriedly away, he left Nancy Drew and her friends in possession of the cottage.

"The idea of his trying to drive us away when he didn't have any right here himself!" Bess exclaimed. "I call that nerve!"

"I was terribly frightened," Alice confessed. "He had such an evil look. I thought for a minute he intended to harm us."

"So did I," George admitted. "I guess Nancy called his bluff."

"I'm not so sure it was all bluff," Nancy observed quietly. "I have a feeling that Zany may try to make trouble for us yet."

"But why?" Alice asked.

"Well, for one thing, I may have been unwise to say what I did about seeing him talking with Martha Frank."

"He did look queer when you said that," George declared. "I think it frightened him."

"What do you suppose he came here for?" Bess demanded. "Do you think Martha really owes him a bill?"

"No, I don't," Nancy returned. "It wouldn't surprise me if he is engaged in some shady business, but what it is I can't make a guess. He seems to have some sort of hold over Martha. I wonder if he has ever been here before?"

As the question occurred to her she stepped

to the bedroom where Lucy had hidden herself.

"It's all right," she told the child. "The man has left. Come on out."

"I saw him through the keyhole," Lucy admitted.

"Tell me, has he ever been here before?"

"Oh, yes, lots of times."

Before Nancy could ask another question, Alice clutched her by the arm.

"Martha is coming up the path! Oh, let's get away before she comes!"

"I'm not afraid to meet her."

"Oh, please let's go," Bess broke in. "It will only be unpleasant."

Giving in to the entreaties, Nancy permitted herself to be pulled toward the back door. They slipped out and were well hidden by the trees by the time Martha reached the cottage. As the girls had tied their ponies at the rear of the cabin, they were able to mount and ride away without attracting attention.

The rain had dwindled to a mere drizzle and long before they reached the ranch the sun was shining as brightly as ever. On the way the girls continued to discuss Zany's strange actions, but for the most part Nancy remained silent, apparently lost in deep thought.

As they drove up to the ranch house, Mrs. Rawley, who was sitting on the porch, got up and came down to meet them. Before the girls could tell her of their little adventure, she made an announcement of her own.

"Girls, I have good news for you. I've been getting my business in shape, and I believe we can start East inside of a week!"

"Good news?" Bess echoed. "That will mean the end of all our good times!"

"You mean you girls have actually enjoyed it out here?" Mrs. Rawley asked. "I thought perhaps you were just trying to be good sports."

"I never had a better time in all my life!" Alice declared, and the others agreed with her.

"I'm sorry we have to leave—just now," Nancy said, and stopped.

Mrs. Rawley glanced at her inquiringly and the girl felt that she was asking for an explanation. Quickly, she told what had occurred at the Martha Frank cottage, and the others added their observations.

"I'm sure there's something wrong at that cabin," Nancy ended, with a troubled frown. "I feel that I've struck the first real clue, too. If we were to remain a few weeks longer I believe I could ferret out the secret! But of course that is impossible."

"Not at all!" Mrs. Rawley declared promptly. "I thought you girls were probably beginning to tire of ranch life, but since you aren't I am in no particular hurry to get back

to Chicago. You go ahead, Nancy, and see
what you can find out."

"Imagine unearthing a mystery this far
from home!" Bess marveled. "Nancy seems
to have a genius for running into them."

"But not for discovering the solution,"
Nancy returned soberly. "So far, I haven't
much to go on. All we know is that something
appears to be wrong at the cottage."

"I'm willing to trust your intuition," George
declared. "It hasn't failed in times past."

Greatly excited at the prospect of being involved in what they termed "a real mystery,"
the girls continued to discuss the various details of their encounter with Zany Shaw. After
a few minutes Nancy slipped away unnoticed
to her room, for she wished to be alone. She
knew that it was time to get down to cases if
she were to make any headway. Time was
short and she must act quickly.

As she began to consider the mystery, it was
not of Zany Shaw that she thought, but of the
child Lucy. Here she was on fairly sure
ground. The child did not appear to be any
relation to Martha Frank, and the doll and the
handsome clothes she had seen in the trunk suggested that perhaps Lucy had belonged to a
good family.

"I feel almost certain those baby dresses
must have been worn by Lucy years ago," she

told herself. "But what objection would Martha have to permitting her to look at them or play with the doll?"

For some minutes Nancy could think of no plausible theory, and then with a flash it came. Kidnapped!

"Oh, pshaw!" she told herself an instant later. "That's a flimsy theory at best. Dad says the first one you think of is seldom the right one. The only trouble is that I can't think of anything else."

Though Nancy continued to wrack her brain, she could not see her way through the maze of miscellaneous information which she had gathered.

"There's probably nothing to that kidnapping idea," she decided at last. "But just for the fun of it I'll assume that there is and see what I can discover. That Philadelphia tag in those baby garments may offer a clue. At any rate I'll telegraph Dad and ask him to have the newspaper and police files in that city searched. I'll ask George Miller to take me to Mougarstown this very night! I can't afford to let any grass grow under my feet!"

CHAPTER XVI

Lost

THOUGH George Miller was not particularly enthusiastic over the prospect of making a special trip to Mougarstown, Nancy's power of persuasion soon won him over. The other girls were invited to go too, but as their excursion into the mountains had left them rather tired, they declined.

Nancy found the telegraph office without difficulty, arriving only a few minutes before it closed. She wrote out a lengthy wire to her father and after some hesitation sent it to River Heights.

"I haven't had a letter from him for nearly a week," she thought, "and it's possible he is now in Canada. In that case my telegram will probably reach him too late to do any good. Oh, I do hope he gets it and is able to find out what I want to know."

Nancy realized that the solution of the mystery would depend in part at least upon the information which must be secured in Philadelphia. Without her father's aid her hands would be tied, for she would not dare to go ahead without definite evidence. To do so might involve her in serious trouble, perhaps a suit for damages.

The following day and the next she waited patiently, knowing that she could not reasonably expect a reply in such a short time. But when two more days had slipped away she became uneasy. Every time the telephone rang she rushed to answer it, hoping that it would be a message from the Mougarstown telegraph office. She was forced to the belief that her father had not received her message after all, for she had stressed the importance of her request. It was not like her father to delay.

"What is the matter with you?" Bess demanded bluntly after Nancy had made another trip to the telephone. "Every time that thing rings you jump a mile! Why, you're as nervous as a cat. You haven't been yourself since that day when we stopped at Martha Frank's to get out of the rain."

"I'm expecting a message from Dad."

"Something about that child Lucy, isn't it?"

Nancy nodded.

"I thought at first we had stumbled upon a mystery," Bess continued. "But since I've been thinking it over I've convinced myself that we were jumping at conclusions. There's nothing so unusual about a trunk of old-fashioned clothes. We have lots of them in our own attic.''

"But you aren't a squatter,'' Nancy returned dryly. "Such children don't have expensive jewelry and elegant lace dresses.''

"That's so,'' Bess admitted.

"It may be as you say that there's nothing wrong at all, but just the same I intend to have another look at that trunk. I'd like to go back to the cottage this afternoon.''

"Oh, not this afternoon,'' Bess protested. "We've planned to go to Chimney Rock, and Alice and George thought to-day would be the best time. Mr. Miller says the colors of the rocks are simply gorgeous.''

"Oh, all right,'' Nancy gave in. "When do we start?''

"The sooner the better. It's a long ride.''

"You round up George and Alice and I'll change into my riding habit.''

While Bess went to find George and Alice, Nancy Drew hurried to her room. By the time she reappeared the others had brought out the ponies and were ready to depart.

"How about lunch?'' Nancy asked.

"We have enough to feed an army,'' Alice told her.

Mrs. Rawley came out to say good-bye to the girls and to ask them what time they would return.

"Probably not before sundown," George told her. "It's a long ride and it may take more time than we expect. Don't worry if we aren't back just on the minute."

"I don't like to have you out after dark."

"Oh, we'll probably be back before that, but if we shouldn't be, don't worry. We're getting to be seasoned mountaineers by this time."

The girls sprang into their saddles and galloped away. George took the lead, for it was she who had planned the trip and consulted Mr. Miller as to the route. As they swung into a canyon, Nancy lost herself in the beauty of the scenery and did not pay a great deal of attention to the trail. However, after they had climbed steadily for perhaps two hours, she began to wish that she had talked with Mr. Miller herself.

"We've branched off from the main trail," she observed. "Are you sure we're going right, George?"

"Yes, Mr. Miller said we turned by a gigantic pine tree."

"We've passed a number of pine trees."

"But only one really big one. I'm sure this is right."

Nancy said no more, for the trail was interesting, and she trusted to George's information. The girls rode on for some time, and then halted for luncheon. They rested longer than they had intended and when they again set off it was nearly three o'clock.

"How much farther is it?" Nancy questioned presently, with a troubled frown.

"We must be getting almost there," George declared. "I had no idea it was so far."

Silently, the girls continued. They had begun to lose their enthusiasm for the trip now that they were getting tired.

"We'll never get back to the ranch by dark," Alice observed presently. "When we do get to Chimney Rock we won't have time for more than a glance—then we'll have to start right back."

"I'm sure we'll get there in a few minutes," George said, but her voice was not as confident as before.

The trail had become steeper and large rocks and stones made it more difficult for the ponies. It was necessary for the girls to watch closely lest their mounts stumble and fall. For perhaps fifteen minutes they continued to climb, then Nancy drew rein.

"George," she said quietly, "are you sure you haven't made a mistake?"

"I'm not sure. I didn't think it was this far."

"I believe we must have taken the wrong trail back there at the first fork."

"I'm afraid we did," George admitted uncomfortably.

"Then the only thing we can do is to start back for the ranch. It's getting late anyway, and we wouldn't have time to see Chimney Rock if we did find the right trail."

"Let's do start back," Bess put in. "If we aren't home by dark, Aunt Nell will worry about us."

Thoroughly discouraged, the girls turned their ponies and began the homeward trip.

"It's all my fault," George mourned as they rode along. "I didn't pay enough attention to what Mr. Miller told me."

"Don't feel badly," Nancy comforted. "Any one of us might have made the same mistake. In fact, it isn't the first time we've missed the trail."

"At least we'll get home for supper," Alice added optimistically.

Nancy glanced toward the west where in a blaze of color the sun was sinking behind a distant peak.

"We'll have to hurry if we do."

Nancy's warning and the thought of warm food served to spur the girls on and for some time they rode in silence. Presently, they came to a fork in the trail and Nancy, who was well in the lead, paused.

"Which way did we come, George?"

George gazed at the two paths in bewilderment.

"Why, I'm not sure. I think we must have come up the left-hand one."

"Oh, it couldn't have been!" Bess broke in. "I'm sure it was the one to the right."

Nancy looked perplexed. She had no idea which trail to take, for they both looked alike. She blamed herself that she had not noted various landmarks, even though George had been leading the party. Dismounting, she led her pony a short way down the right-hand path, examining the trail for hoof marks.

"The ground is too hard and rocky," she complained. "There isn't a sign of a print."

"There isn't on the other trail either," George informed her gloomily.

"Then I vote we take the right-hand path," Bess suggested.

Since there was no opposition to the proposal, Nancy mounted her pony again and led the way. As they descended into the canyon, she kept searching for familiar landmarks, but saw none.

"We seem to be going in the right direction," she admitted in response to Bess's anxious inquiry, "but, someway, I have a feeling we took the wrong trail."

Before they had continued very far this feeling became a firm conviction, but as the others were inclined to believe they were on the right trail, she hesitated to set her judgment up against theirs.

"We should have passed that big pine tree long ago," she observed presently.

Of one accord the girls halted their ponies and surveyed their surroundings. Already the evening shadows were settling over the canyon; in less than an hour it would be dark.

"Nancy is right," George admitted reluctantly. "We must have made another mistake. What shall we do? Go back?"

"It will be dark before we could reach the fork," Bess protested. "Why not go on? At least we are going in the right direction and we're bound to come out somewhere near the ranch."

"That sounds logical," George observed. "What do you think, Nancy?"

"It seems to me we ought to go back."

"But as long as we're traveling in the right direction——"

"Which direction do you think we are going?" Nancy asked quietly.

"Why, east of course."

"We're going almost straight south," Bess declared.

Nancy smiled grimly.

"I'm afraid we're all hopelessly mixed up.

That's why I think we should turn back.''

The others were convinced of her wisdom, and without a word began to retrace their way. Their uncertainty about the directions had shaken their confidence.

Long before they reached the fork in the trail it was dark. Though the stars were out, there was no moon to guide them, and the girls rode close together as though for mutual protection. Reaching the branch-off, they selected the left-hand path, but before they had gone a half mile, Nancy called a halt.

''Girls,'' she said, and there was a slight tremor in her voice, ''there's no use going any farther.''

''What do you mean?'' Alice asked shakily.

''I don't believe this is the right trail either. We must have made our mistake farther up the mountain.''

''Then we're—'' George broke off, unwilling to put her thoughts into words.

''Yes, we may as well admit the truth.'' Nancy's voice carried finality. ''We're hopelessly lost!''

CHAPTER XVII

A Night of Horror

Lost! The very word struck Nancy Drew and her friends with terror. Frequently the girls had been warned that they would lose their way among the labyrinth of twisting, branching trails, but so confident had they grown that they had discounted the risk. Now, with all their hearts, they wished that they had paid more attention to the route.

"Perhaps if we give the ponies free rein, they'll know enough to go home," George suggested.

"We can try it," Nancy said doubtfully.

As she spoke she dropped the reins over the neck of her pony, and directed the animal: "Go home, Marcus!"

The pony turned its head as though to ask her what she meant by abandoning the reins, but remained motionless. Impatiently, Nancy gave him a slap on the flank. To her disappointment, Marcus then ambled down the path which the girls had just decided could not be the right one.

"It's no use," she declared, reining her mount in.

"The ponies would start off for the ranch fast enough if we didn't want them to," George complained. "If only an old lynx would come along to scare them!"

"George, how can you joke at a time like this?" Bess demanded, almost tearfully. "It gives me the creeps to think what may become of us."

George sobered instantly for she realized all too keenly the serious predicament which they faced.

"Forgive me! I know it's no laughing matter."

Darkness had crept swiftly upon the mountain and with it came a chill wind which penetrated the light clothing worn by the girls. Alice shivered and glanced inquiringly toward Nancy as though to ask her what they were to do.

Sensing that the morale of the group was about to break, Nancy Drew knew that she must assume definite leadership. Though her own courage was at low ebb, she must not disclose by word or action that she feared the worst.

"At least we have the revolver and plenty of ammunition," she observed as cheerfully as possible. "We'll be safe from wild animals."

"What are we to do?" Bess demanded

bluntly. "We can't stay here and wait for a searching party that may never come. I'm freezing to death already."

"I think we had best keep on the move," Nancy told her. "Surely, we will find the trail soon."

Though she spoke confidently, Nancy had little faith in her own words. In the dark she had lost all sense of direction, and one trail appeared little different from another. Only chance could take them safely back to Shadow Ranch.

Soberly, the girls set off down one of the paths which appeared the most promising. They rode close together and did not talk. Several times Alice and Bess glanced apprehensively over their shoulders as they heard some unusual sound in the bush.

"I'm nearly starved," George declared after a time. "Did we eat up all of those sandwiches?"

"The last one," Bess replied gloomily. "Just think what we must have missed at the ranch. Maybe baked ham or steak and hot biscuits, coffee——"

"Don't try to tantalize us!" Nancy begged.

The girls rode on for a time, more slowly than before as their ponies were beginning to tire.

Presently there came the weird hoot of an

owl almost in their ears. Alice jumped and shuddered. Then from a distance came the sharp bark of a fox. Later, but from afar, the cry of a wildcat reached their ears. All about them they could hear the rustle of night animals in search of their prey, but nothing came within their sight.

"Don't you suppose the folks at the ranch have a searching party out looking for us by this time?" asked George after a while.

"I hope so," Nancy returned. "But you remember we told Mrs. Rawley not to worry if we didn't get back until late."

"I know. That's the bad part of it. By the time they decide we're lost anything may have happened."

"I believe we're safe as long as we keep a sharp watch for wild animals. We can keep moving——"

"I can't very much longer," Alice said in a strained voice. "I'm so tired and cold."

"You poor thing!" Nancy halted in the trail and stripped off her sweater. "Here, take this. I don't need it."

"I won't take your sweater. Why, you're shivering yourself."

In spite of Nancy's urging, Alice remained steadfast in her decision not to take the sweater. However, it was plain to the others that the girl was going on her nerve alone. Her face was pale and drawn and her teeth chattered continually.

"She's nearly ready to collapse," Nancy told herself. "We can't keep on."

Already she was convinced that they were stranded on the mountain for the night. Glancing at her watch she was surprised to note the hour.

"Why, it's nearly midnight!" she exclaimed. "We've been wandering around half the night."

"I had no idea it was so late," George admitted, "even though I do feel as if I've been in the saddle for a week."

"Girls," and Nancy spoke with decision, "we may as well admit that we're not getting anywhere. This trail we're following seems to lead deeper into the mountains instead of back to the ranch. I think the best thing we can do is to call a halt and wait until daylight before we try to go on."

There was a long moment of silence as the girls considered Nancy's suggestion. They knew that her plan was the wisest, and yet it frightened them to think that they must spend the remainder of the night in the woods in the midst of the ghostly rustlings and night sounds. George was the first to speak.

"You're right, Nancy. It's the only thing to do. We must try to get a little sleep."

"Sleep!" Bess wailed. "Do you think I could close my eyes with all these wild creatures ready to pounce upon me the minute I did?"

"We can take turns keeping watch," Nancy observed quietly. "Now if we can only find a likely-looking place where we shall be protected from the wind at least!"

Dismounting, she led her pony toward a rocky ledge not far from the trail.

"This cliff ought to break the wind," she called to the others. "Hello? What's this?" Before her friends could reach her, she gave a little cry of pleasure. "Girls, we're in luck! I've found a cave."

The others hurried up, but only George shared Nancy's enthusiasm for the discovery. Alice and Bess refused to peep in at the opening in the ledge.

"It looks like a bear cave to me," Bess cried anxiously. "Oh, let's hunt for another place."

"You can't tell a bear cave by the outside," Nancy returned, with a laugh. "It seems a shame to go away and leave this place. Inside we would be warm and snug until morning. We could barricade ourselves and keep out any wild animals that might come prowling about."

"Nancy Drew, you'll be killed if you go into that cave," Bess insisted, her eyes wide with fright. "I just know there's a bear inside!"

Nancy hesitated. In all truth she was not

especially eager to investigate the cave, for she realized that it could easily be inhabited by wild animals. She listened intently, but no sound issued from within.

"It's safe enough!" she declared. "Here's for it!"

"I'll go with you," George encouraged her. "Have you your revolver ready?"

The girls were without a flashlight, and as Nancy cautiously thrust her head into the cave she could see nothing at first. Then gradually her eyes became accustomed to the dark. She saw to her relief that she was in a small chamber, and apparently it was not inhabited.

Inch by inch Nancy and George explored the cave. As soon as they were convinced that it was safe they called to Alice and Bess, but it was necessary to do a great deal of coaxing before the two girls timidly crawled inside.

"We must barricade the entrance with rocks and brush," Nancy announced.

The girls had already unsaddled and tied their ponies securely to a tree not far from the entrance of the cave, and as soon as they had collected a huge pile of rocks and thorn brush, were ready to turn in.

"This isn't half bad," Nancy declared as they settled themselves for the night. "We're warm and cosy and that's something to be thankful for."

"Do you think we'll be safe?" Bess inquired nervously.

"It would take a vicious animal to break through our barricade. However, to make certain that we're not disturbed, we can take turns watching. George and I can sit up two hours and then you and Alice can relieve us."

As this plan met with approval, Alice and Bess stretched themselves out on the hard floor of the cave and were soon asleep. For a half hour Nancy and George kept their watch faithfully, but as no sound other than the calling of night birds and the distant sound of foraging animals disturbed the tranquillity of the night, they began to grow sleepy. George caught herself dozing several times. Presently, her head dropped lower and she slept.

Nancy, glancing toward her friend, smiled. She knew that George was tired and needed the rest.

"I'll not awaken her," she decided. "There's no need for more than one to stand guard."

At first Nancy Drew experienced no trouble in keeping awake, but as the time dragged slowly on, she found it increasingly difficult to remain alert. Without realizing it, she began to nod.

Then all at once she was wide awake again. Something had startled her. What was it?

She tried to pierce the darkness, but could see nothing. Could she have been mistaken? Then she heard the ponies move restlessly and one of them neigh shrilly.

Just as she was settling back against the wall, she heard another sound. This time there could be no mistake. The noise came from the entrance of the cave!

CHAPTER XVIII

SAFE AGAIN

NANCY DREW grew tense with fright as she heard the sound at the mouth of the cave and for a moment she could not move. A wild animal had rubbed against the brush used to barricade the entrance and was sniffing suspiciously. Nervously, Nancy gripped her revolver and crept forward.

To her intense relief, she found that there was no need to use the weapon, for already the animal had moved away, evidently discouraged by the sharp thorns which barred the opening to the cave. After making certain that the animal had left, Nancy moved back to her place against the wall.

She glanced toward her three companions and saw that they were sleeping peacefully. There was no need to disturb them. For perhaps another hour she kept watch faithfully, but there was no further cause for alarm. Then, fearing that she could not keep her eyes open much longer, she decided to awaken Bess

and Alice. Already it was long past the time
assigned for their watch.

Accordingly, she awakened the two girls, but
wisely said nothing of the animal that had tried
to enter the cave, knowing that it would only
frighten them.

As soon as she had been relieved, Nancy
stretched herself out on the hard ground and
was soon lost in slumber. She did not awaken
until the morning sun streamed into the cave.

"Get up!" George told her. "Breakfast is
ready!"

"Breakfast!" Nancy smiled wanly.

"No joking. While we were sleeping, Bess
and Alice went out and picked wild berries."

After eating the fruit and drinking at a
spring which they found not far from the cave
and looking after the ponies, Nancy and her
friends took stock of the situation. Now that
it was daylight, their predicament seemed less
serious.

"We at least know our directions," Nancy
observed, glancing toward the rising sun. "I
believe we were going around in circles most
of the time last night."

After considering the various trails, the girls
selected one which they had not traveled the
previous evening, and set off hopefully. Presently, they came to a mountain stream and
after permitting their ponies to drink, fol-

lowed a trail which led along its winding banks.

"I'm sure we didn't come this way," Nancy declared, "but we're going in the right direction and I think we'll come out somewhere near the ranch before we've traveled very far."

"I'm hungry enough to eat a fried rock," Bess remarked. "Those berries just whetted my appetite."

The trail which the girls were following appeared to be well traveled, and as the morning sun rose higher, they became more hopeful. Surely they would meet someone from one of the ranches before long, they told themselves. Undoubtedly, a party had been sent out from Shadow Ranch to search for them, and it would be only a matter of hours until they would be found.

Then unexpectedly they caught a flash of color in the bushes some distance ahead. At first they could not believe their eyes, but as they urged their ponies faster, they saw a girl with a pail over her arm, picking berries not far from the stream. Seeing the strangers, she retreated into the bushes, but Nancy called to her.

"Don't run away!"

A timid pair of eyes peeped out through the bushes and then the grimy face of the child relaxed into a grin. It was Lucy Brown.

"Hello!" Nancy greeted her. "What are you doing here? You aren't lost too?"

"Lost?" Lucy demanded with a scornful toss of her head. "I know every trail on this mountain."

"Then perhaps you can tell us how to get back to Shadow Ranch."

"Don't you know where you are? You're only about a mile from our cottage. It's over that way."

Lucy indicated the direction with a jerk of her thumb.

"You can get back to the ranch that way, or I can tell you how to take a short cut."

"We'll take the shortest way," Nancy told her. "We can't get back too quickly."

Lucy hesitated, apparently groping for words which would most clearly identify the route.

"I'll walk along with you for a way," she decided, "and then you can't make a mistake."

Nancy took her up on Marcus and smiled at the child's delight. Though she had lived many years in the mountains, this was the first time she had ever ridden horseback.

"Won't your—" Nancy struggled for the right word—"your guardian worry about you?"

"Oh, she doesn't care what I do just so I don't talk with folks." Lucy glanced up guiltily. "Why won't she let me have anything to do with other girls?"

The question startled Nancy and left her at a loss for a reply. Why indeed? If only she knew! She glanced down at Lucy with compassion.

"How would you like to come to Shadow Ranch to live?" she asked upon impulse.

Lucy's face lighted up.

"Oh, it would be wonderful! But I can't. *She* wouldn't let me."

"Perhaps I could talk with her and convince her that it would be the best thing to do."

"If only you could! But there's no use hoping. I know she won't let me come."

"I'll talk with her, anyway."

"When? To-day?"

"Perhaps to-morrow. We are in a hurry to get back to Shadow Ranch now. We've been lost in the mountains all night and we haven't had anything to eat."

"Why didn't you say so before?" Lucy thrust out her half-filled berry pail reproachfully. "Here, take these."

"We'll pay you for the fruit."

"It wouldn't do any good. Martha would just take it away from me."

Nancy accepted the pail gratefully and after taking out a handful of berries, passed it on to the others. They soon reached a point where two trails branched off.

"This is as far as I'll go," Lucy announced. "Just keep following the one to the right and it will take you straight to the ranch."

Thanking Lucy for her help, the girls said good-bye and continued on their way. Nancy was very thoughtful as she rode along, for more than ever before she realized how great was the child's need of home and a responsible guardian. She really meant what she had said about bringing Lucy to Shadow Ranch, though she had spoken upon impulse.

"It will not be easy to bring Martha Frank around to my way of thinking," she told herself, "but I believe I can do it if I threaten her with the authorities. I'll go and see her the first thing to-morrow. If only that telegram from Father has arrived while I have been away! It may strengthen my position."

At this moment the girls emerged from the timber and saw Shadow Ranch only a short distance away. The sight drove all thought of Lucy Brown from Nancy's mind and her only desire was to reach the ranch as quickly as possible.

"The place looks deserted," Alice observed as they approached. "I wonder what has become of everyone?"

"They're probably out searching for us," George laughed.

She could afford to laugh now that the danger was over. As the girls rode toward the barn, the ranch house door swung open and Mrs. Rawley and Mrs. Miller rushed out to meet the girls.

"Oh, I've been worried half to death," Mrs. Rawley cried. "How thankful I am you are back safe and sound. Mr. Miller and the boys are out looking for you now!"

Quickly, and most contritely, the girls related what had happened to them.

"You poor dears," Mrs. Miller declared when they had finished. "You must be half starved. I'll get you something right away. I've got a berry shortcake baking in the oven this minute."

The girls exchanged quick glances.

"Please," George ventured, "if you don't mind, could we have the shortcake without the berries?"

Mrs. Miller stared at the girls rather blankly and then she began to chuckle.

"I might have known you wouldn't want the berries."

With that she hurried toward the kitchen, but before she could enter the ranch house, Nancy ran after her.

"Oh, Mrs. Miller," she said in a low voice,

"while I was away did a telegram come for me?"

"Nothing came."

Nancy turned away in disappointment. What could it mean? Had her father failed to get her message? Probably he had already gone to Canada, and the telegram had not been forwarded to him. If only she could hear from him before she went to see Martha Frank!

CHAPTER XIX

A Surprise

Nancy Drew did not forget her promise to Lucy Brown. The following morning she spoke to Mrs. Rawley about bringing the child to Shadow Ranch for a few days.

"If I can get her away from that woman I may be able to learn something which will throw light on her parentage," she declared.

"By all means bring her here if Martha Frank will give permission," Mrs. Rawley assured her. "From what you have told me I know that poor child will appreciate a good home and kind treatment. We'll all do what we can for her."

Directly after breakfast Nancy set off for the cottage alone. She had invited the other girls to accompany her, but they were too tired and battered from their experience of the previous days to show any enthusiasm.

"Do be careful," Mrs. Rawley warned her as Nancy rode away. "That woman is such an odd creature—there's no telling what she may do if she becomes angry."

"I'll try to be diplomatic with her."

Nancy was not afraid of Martha Frank, yet, as she headed toward the cottage, she realized that her mission would not be a pleasant one. She tried to think out what she could say to the woman to convince her that it was wisest to send Lucy away.

"I can't appeal to her through a sense of justice to the child," she thought, "for she doesn't care a whit what becomes of her."

She was still considering the problem when she rode up to the cottage. Of course, she could threaten Martha, but she had little evidence to substantiate any accusation she might make. If only she had heard from her father!

Tying her pony she walked up to the cottage and then stopped short in amazement. The front door was open, permitting Nancy a glimpse of the interior. To her surprise, everything was in confusion. Two trunks had been dragged out into the kitchen and were half filled with articles of apparel and household goods. Boxes were filled with cooking utensils and other odds and ends.

As Nancy stopped aghast, Martha Frank, who was bending over one of the boxes, straightened and stared blankly at the girl.

"You're not moving?" Nancy asked quickly.

Martha nodded grimly.

"It looks like it, don't it?"

"You're leaving the country?"

"What's it to you where I'm goin'?"

"A great deal. You see, I came over to ask you if Lucy couldn't stay with me at the ranch for a few days."

"No, she can't," the woman snapped. "Lucy goes with me."

"But——"

"Lucy goes with me and that's all there is to it."

The lines of Nancy's face tightened. How thoroughly she disliked this woman who eyed her with such distrust! She must manage to have her way about Lucy, but what could she do?

"If it's money you want—" she began.

A gleam of interest shone in Martha's eyes, but she shook her head firmly.

"What you so interested in Lucy for?"

As Nancy studied the woman, it seemed to her that there was fear as well as suspicion behind the question. She must take care how she answered.

"I've taken a fancy to her. Yesterday when I was lost in the mountains she showed me the way home. I would like to do something for her."

"There ain't anything you kin do. I tell you Lucy's going with me."

"What right have you to take her?" Nancy

demanded somewhat sharply, for she was growing impatient. "Is she your child?"

"It's none of your business."

"It is if I care to make it! I am convinced that Lucy is no relation to you, and unless you can produce papers showing that you are her legal guardian, I will not permit you to take her away!"

Nancy had spoken boldly, but in her own mind she was not certain she could carry out her threat. For an instant she believed that her bluff had been effective, for Martha cringed, but in another instant a defiant smile played over the woman's face.

"You can't do a thing to me!" she retorted. "I have friends who will look after me if you try to stir up trouble."

"You mean that old junk dealer?"

Martha did not respond, but, turning her back, continued with the packing. Nancy knew that she had accomplished nothing. Why was the woman so stubborn? It was disheartening, but she would not give up. She continued to plead and to coax. The woman did not pay the slightest attention to what she said, and would not answer any of the questions put to her. At last, tiring of the monologue, Nancy left the cottage.

As she rode slowly toward Shadow Ranch, she tried to think of a new method of attack.

She was more determined than ever that Martha should not take Lucy away, but she was at her wit's end. What could she do?

"I'd like to know why she is leaving so unexpectedly," Nancy thought. "I'll venture it's because she thinks I'll find out something about that child! She's always been afraid to have me talk with her."

The more she considered the matter, the more she realized the importance of preventing Martha from leaving the country. All trace of Lucy would then be lost, and she would never have an opportunity to examine the clothing and jewelry in the old trunk.

"If only I could get another look at it!" she told herself. "It might help clear up the mystery!"

Nancy had never felt more helpless in her life. It seemed to her that just as she was about to make an important discovery, fate had intervened. But was it fate? No, she decided, Martha's leave-taking was a deliberate affair. Was it not possible that she had been warned to go by Zany Shaw? Certainly the man exerted a power over the woman, and he had seen Nancy and her friends at the cottage. Martha's decision to leave had followed so swiftly upon the encounter with the junk man that it appeared not unlikely that there was some connection. But why was Zany Shaw concerned with Martha Frank? It all seemed a hopeless muddle.

As she rode up to the corral, George Miller came out of the barn to unsaddle her pony. Feeling the need of advice, Nancy decided to tell the foreman of her experience.

"Martha Frank is moving away," she began.

"Pshaw, you're joking," George grinned. "Old Martha wouldn't have enough cash to move her duds to Mougarstown."

"She must have acquired it somewhere. I went over to see her about having Lucy come here to stay, and she had nearly all of her things packed then. Oh, Mr. Miller, can't you help me? I must get that child out of her clutches, and I'm desperate!"

The foreman scratched his head thoughtfully. Though he still pretended an indifference toward the girls, especially George Fayne whose name he had never acknowledged, he had a sincere regard and respect for Nancy.

"I don't know what you can do," he said at last. "But Martha oughtn't to be allowed to get away with that kid."

"Couldn't we get some of the ranch folk interested in the case?"

"Most of them will be only too glad to see her go."

"But with Lucy it is different."

"People don't know much about her, and

knowing that she belongs to Martha they wouldn't want to do anything.''

''Then I can't look to anyone but myself for help?''

''That's about the size of it.   Course, if I can help you I will, but I don't see what can be done.''

''Neither do I—now,'' Nancy said, as she walked away. ''But I'll find a way! I won't give up!''

CHAPTER XX

A MOONLIGHT RIDE

"OH, Nancy, guess who called while you were away?" Bess Marvin ran down the walk to meet her friend as she came up from the corrals after talking with the foreman.

"It wasn't from the telegraph office?" Nancy demanded eagerly.

"No, it was one of your admirers."

"My admirers?"

"Yes, Doctor Cole."

"Pooh! I think he's more interested in Alice than he is in me. What did he want?"

"He wants to get up a riding party for to-night. There's to be David Glaston and Alice's friend from the Bar X and that young man who took a fancy to George. I've forgotten his name."

"You talk as though it were all settled."

"Well, it is—practically. They especially wanted to go to-night because there's a full moon. We had to come to a decision, and since you weren't here—you do want to go, don't you?" This anxiously.

Nancy hesitated and then smiled reassuringly.

Had the choice been left to her she would have selected any night but the present. However, she could not bear to disappoint the others, and after all it was unlikely that she would be able to do anything to prevent Martha Frank from departing.

"Yes, I think it will be lots of fun," she told Bess.

All afternoon Nancy was silent and preoccupied. The others were sympathetic when they learned what was troubling her, but the prospect of a moonlight ride so thrilled them that it was difficult for them to take the matter as seriously as she did.

"I'm afraid I can't help you," Mrs. Rawley confessed when Nancy asked her for advice. "I don't know of any way you can get the child unless you take her by force."

"But could I hold her that way? Martha might send the authorities here."

"They say the child has been mistreated. If that is true, Martha Frank isn't fit to be her guardian."

"I am sure she has abused Lucy, but unfortunately I haven't any proof of it."

"Whatever you decide to do, I'll stand behind you," Mrs. Rawley promised. "When is this Frank woman leaving?"

"I don't know, but probably not before tomorrow or the next day."

"Then you can drive over to-morrow and
see her again. I'll go with you. Perhaps together we can do something with her."

"Oh, thank you," Nancy said gratefully. "I
knew you'd help me."

It was with an easier mind that she prepared
for the evening ride. By eight o'clock Doctor
Cole and his party had arrived and the girls
were ready to start.

"I feel certain you'll get back safe and sound
this time," Mrs. Rawley laughed as she said
good-bye. "With four protectors who are thoroughly acquainted with the country, you haven't
a chance of losing yourselves."

The young people cantered off down the
road, Nancy and Doctor Cole taking the lead.

"I thought we could follow this trail as far
as Martha Frank's cabin," the young doctor
suggested. "Then we can cut off through the
mountains and take the Granville road back to
the ranch. It's very beautiful that way. Does
the plan suit you?"

"Perfectly."

Nancy was indeed pleased that they were to
ride past Martha's cottage, for it would give
her an opportunity to make certain that the
woman had not yet departed. In spite of her
troubled thoughts about Lucy, she managed to
maintain a light conversation and Doctor Cole
did not notice her preoccupation.

Presently, the party drew near the cottage and Nancy was relieved to see smoke curling up from the chimney. That meant that Martha was still there.

She would have ridden by the cabin without stopping had she not caught sight of a man standing in the doorway. In her surprise, Nancy involuntarily halted her pony, and Doctor Cole drew up beside her.

"What is the matter?" he questioned.

Nancy did not answer. Her eyes were riveted upon the man in the doorway. As he saw her looking at him, he gave a little start and moved back into the shadow.

It was Zany Shaw. Nancy Drew's face became grim as she recognized him.

"What—?" Doctor Cole began, but the question died on his lips.

A piercing cry rang out and there was a commotion in the bushes at the rear of the cottage. With one accord, Nancy and her friends turned to look.

To their amazement they saw Lucy Brown dart out of the bushes. She was pursued by Martha Frank, who wielded a big stick and shouted ugly threats. So intent was the woman upon capturing the child that she failed to see the young people who had halted in the shadow of a big tree.

"Stop that!" Nancy shouted angrily, urging

her pony forward. "Don't you dare strike her!"

Martha was too far away to hear the words, but the sound of hoof beats caused her to wheel around. She saw Nancy, with Doctor Cole only a short distance behind, bearing down upon her. In consternation she dropped the stick.

Lucy, unaware that Martha had given up the chase, continued to run as one possessed, making straight for a clump of bushes which fringed a small cliff at the rear of the cottage. In her frightened state, the child did not seem to be aware of where she was going or of the danger which threatened.

In horror, Nancy tried to warn her.

"Stop!" she cried frantically. "The cliff!"

Lucy cast a quick glance over her shoulder but did not slacken her speed. Before Nancy could cry out again, the child stumbled upon a stone in the path. In an effort to save herself from a fall, she clutched at the bushes. For an instant she maintained her hold, but as the weight of her body was thrown forward, the frail branches snapped. Lucy gave a scream of terror and tried desperately for a new hold, but failed. The ground beneath her crumbled, and she fell headlong over the cliff.

There came a thud and a rattling of stones as she struck the bottom.

CHAPTER XXI

The Accident

Even as Lucy Brown plunged over the side of the cliff, Nancy Drew leaped from her pony and ran forward. Quick as was her action, Doctor Cole was but a few steps behind her. They reached the brink of the cliff, and, tearing aside the bushes, descended the steep slope as rapidly as they dared.

In the dim moonlight they could make out a huddled figure at the bottom of the cliff, but there was not the slightest movement or sound to indicate that Lucy lived.

"Oh, I'm afraid she's—" Nancy stifled the word which came to her lips. Lucy could not be dead, she told herself. It would be too cruel, too unfair.

They reached the child together, and Doctor Cole picked her up in his arms.

"Are we too late?"

"Unconscious but still breathing," the doctor told her. "I can't tell how seriously she is injured. We must get her to the house."

They hurried to a less precipitous part of

the cliff and carried the child up the slope as
gently as possible. Martha Frank would have
rushed out and snatched Lucy from them had
not David Glaston, who had hurried up with
Bess and the other members of the party, re-
strained her by physical force.

"What right have you to come here and interfere?" the woman shrieked hysterically.

Still holding the unconscious Lucy in his
arms, Doctor Cole faced Martha with cold fury.

"Does it mean nothing to you that this child
might have been killed, and at your hand?"

The woman cringed and for the first time saw
how white Lucy's face was. She shrank away
in terror.

With Nancy and the others following, Doctor
Cole stalked toward the cottage. Reaching the
doorway, he found it blocked by Zany Shaw.

"Hand over that child and then git out!"
the junk dealer commanded sharply.

"What have you to do with her?" Nancy
cried impatiently. "She isn't your child."

"You haven't any right to come here," Zany
snarled without answering the question put to
him. "That kid deserved a beating, and she's
going to git it!"

"Oh, she is? Well, we may have something
to say about that!" Doctor Cole brushed past
the man and the others followed him into the
kitchen.

He placed Lucy gently on the couch. Without waiting for orders, Nancy rushed to the cupboard for an extra oil lamp and then set a pan of water on the stove to boil.

Doctor Cole nodded approvingly. With practiced hands he examined the child while the others anxiously awaited his verdict.

"A broken arm seems to be the most apparent of her injuries," he observed. "If I can find something to use for a splint I'll be able to set it here. I don't think her unconsciousness indicates anything grave. She'll soon come out of that."

"I'll see what I can find outside," David Glaston offered.

He returned in a few minutes with a smooth, narrow board which Doctor Cole declared would serve as a splint until a more satisfactory one could be secured. By the time he had set the broken bone, Lucy had regained consciousness.

"Don't let her get me," she begged piteously, clinging to Nancy's hand.

"There, dear, don't worry," Nancy told her gently. "We're going to take you with us to Shadow Ranch."

"What's that?" Zany Shaw demanded, stepping forward. Until now, he had remained in the background, cowed by Doctor Cole's professional attitude.

"I said we were taking Lucy with us to Shadow Ranch," Nancy repeated evenly.

"Not much you ain't! She'll not stir from this house!"

Nancy stared at the man coldly.

"What right have you to give commands?" she asked.

Zany's eyes fell, but he had no intention of admitting defeat. He turned to Martha who had entered the kitchen unobserved by the others.

"Are you going to let them take Lucy to Shadow Ranch?" he demanded.

"No!" she cried defiantly. "You can't take her!"

For answer, Doctor Cole gathered Lucy up in his arms and carried her out, Nancy and the others following. Martha and Zany Shaw came running after them, threatening and pleading.

"If someone will lead my horse, I can carry Lucy," Doctor Cole said briskly, ignoring the two trouble-makers. "I don't believe the ride will hurt her."

"I'll have the law on you if you take that child!" Zany insisted angrily. "Give her to me!"

"Get out of the way!" David Glaston cried impatiently, giving the man a shove.

Zany started toward the cottage.

"I'll make you give her to me! I'll get the shotgun!"

Now somewhat alarmed, for they did not know to what lengths the pair might go, Nancy and her friends hastily mounted their ponies and rode away. Doctor Cole carried Lucy so carefully that she was in no discomfort. It was a slow trip back to the ranch, but at last they arrived.

Lucy was put to bed immediately and after a few minutes she fell asleep. Nancy then joined the others on the veranda to consider what should be done about Martha and Zany Shaw.

"That man has no legal right to interfere," David Glaston declared. "If he makes trouble, just send for me."

"I can't understand why he was so insistent that we leave Lucy at the cottage," Nancy mused. "There is something queer about it. I half believe that it was he who gave Martha the money to move away with."

"If she leaves now it must be without the child," Doctor Cole said firmly. "Lucy can't be moved for at least two weeks. She has suffered severe shock, and while I believe she has escaped internal injury, I can't be certain until I have had her under observation."

"If Martha and that queer man make trouble, we'll all help you," Mrs. Rawley told Nancy. "After to-night's incident, you surely have enough evidence to prove that Martha isn't fit to be her guardian."

Nancy glanced inquiringly at David Glaston.

"Any court would award her to you," he declared. "It was no fault of Martha Frank's that the child wasn't killed, and she seemed utterly lacking in affection."

After perhaps a half hour, the young men said good-bye to the girls and took their departure.

"I'll drive out to see Lucy to-morrow," Doctor Cole promised. "Of course, if she doesn't seem to be in a normal condition, call me."

"What a grand smash to our moonlight ride," Bess sighed after the young men had left. "Oh, well, it was fortunate that we happened to pass Martha's cottage when we did; otherwise, there's no telling what might have been Lucy's fate."

As the girls arose to go into the house, Mrs. Rawley thought of something and called Nancy back.

"I intended to tell you at once," she apologized, "but in the excitement it slipped my mind. While you were gone, one of our neighbors dropped in. He was in Mougarstown this afternoon and it seems the telegraph office asked him to deliver a message to you. I guess the office has been trying to telephone all day, but something must be the matter with the wire.''

"A telegram?" Nancy questioned eagerly. "Oh, I wonder if it's from Dad?"

"I laid the envelope on the desk."

Nancy waited for no more but hurried into the ranch house. If only the message provided the information which she sought!

"I feel certain it will contain news that will throw light on the mystery," she told herself. "If not, it will be the first time Dad ever failed me."

CHAPTER XXII

The Telegram

EAGERLY, Nancy caught up the yellow envelope which lay on the desk and ripped it open. She saw at a glance that it was from her father. The message was a lengthy one and it took her several minutes to read it, but when she had finished a triumphant smile lighted up her face.

"Girls," she called, "come here quick! Just listen to this!"

George and Alice, who had slipped into the kitchen to rummage for something to eat before going to bed, promptly answered the summons as did Mrs. Rawley and Bess, who had not yet, retired.

"Girls, you know I've been working on the theory that Lucy may have been kidnapped," Nancy began. "That Philadelphia tag in those garments we found was my first real clue. I telegraphed Dad and asked him to search the police and newspaper files at Philadelphia. I just heard from him."

"What did he say?" Alice inquired.

"It seems he had a great deal of trouble get-

ting the information I wanted, and that was
why he didn't answer my wire sooner."

"But what did he learn?" George demanded
impatiently. "Don't keep us in suspense."

"First of all, he tried to trace down the firm
of Goodman and Goodman—you remember that
was the name on the dress tag. It seems the
firm went out of business four years ago, so
of course he couldn't learn anything from that
source."

"You delight in keeping us dangling, don't
you?" Bess protested. "We'll die of nervous
prostration if you don't tell us pretty soon what
you've discovered!"

"I'm getting to it as fast as I can. Dad next
made a search of the police files. There was
only one case which appeared at all likely, a
kidnapping which took place some years ago—
eight to be exact. At least, it was thought that
the child was kidnapped, though the truth was
never learned."

"What child?" Bess asked.

"Her name was Louise Bowen, a child of
three and a half years. She mysteriously disappeared from her father's house and it was
believed that she was taken by a discharged
furnace man who sought to avenge himself.
There was never any trace of her found, though
a large reward was offered for her return or
for information leading to her whereabouts."

"What became of the furnace man?" Alice questioned. "Couldn't the police trace him?"

"Father didn't say, but I assume that he too vanished. That gave credence to the theory that it was he who kidnapped the child."

"How old did you say the little girl was at the time of the kidnapping?" Mrs. Rawley inquired.

"Three and a half."

"And she disappeared eight years ago. That would make her nearly twelve now."

Nancy nodded.

"The same age as Lucy Brown," she declared significantly.

"Do you believe Louise Bowen and Lucy are the same?" George asked.

"That's what I don't know. Your guess is as good as mine."

"I'm not so sure about that," George laughed. "You have a way of backing up your theories with sound judgment. But tell me, why did Louise Bowen's parents give up the search for this furnace man?"

"The search was kept up for several years. Mrs. Bowen died three years after Louise disappeared, and then only two years after that Mr. Bowen was killed in a traffic accident. A large fortune was left to Louise, with the stipulation that if she was not found within five years after her father's death, the money was to be distributed among charity institutions. If Louise appears to claim the fortune within two years, it will be hers."

"What a wonderful thing it would be if Lucy were really Louise Bowen," Alice mused.

"Yes," Nancy agreed. "But we're only hoping that such is the case. We must have definite proof before we make any claims. There's one weak link in the chain already."

"What is that?" Mrs. Rawley questioned.

"If Lucy were really Louise Bowen, it seems probable that her kidnappers would have destroyed all evidence pertaining to her identity."

"Meaning that doll and the clothes you saw in the trunk?"

"Exactly. Of course, they may have been too stupid to think of that."

"What do you mean to do?" Alice asked.

"I intend to have another look at that trunk."

"But how can you with Martha in the cottage all the time?"

"I don't know; but I'll find a way!"

After discussing the telegram for some time, the girls went to bed. Before retiring, Nancy stepped into Lucy's bedroom, but the child was sleeping so peacefully that she decided there was no need to sit up with her. However, she left the door which opened into her own bedroom ajar, that she might hear the slightest disturbance.

Twice Nancy arose during the night to make certain that Lucy was not in pain, and so it was that toward morning she fell into a heavy slumber and did not awaken until George nudged her in the ribs.

"Get up, Nancy!" she commanded. "Martha Frank is here to make trouble!"

"Who?" Nancy inquired sleepily.

As George repeated the name Nancy was instantly awake.

"She demands that we give Lucy up to her. Mrs. Rawley told her we wouldn't do it, but she won't go away. She just hangs around the house. We think she intends to watch her chance and steal Lucy away."

Hastily, Nancy Drew began to dress.

"Don't mind Martha," she told George. "Just stay in the house and see that she doesn't get her hands on Lucy."

"What do you mean to do?" George asked, for she saw the glint of determination in Nancy's eyes.

"I'm going straight to the cottage while I have the chance. This is my opportunity to look at that trunk."

"What if Martha sees you go?"

"She's out in front now, isn't she? I'll sneak

out the back way. If she starts to return to the cottage before I get back, you can use some excuse to delay her.''

"It's risky for you," George protested.

"It's the only way I'll ever get the evidence I need. I'm not afraid of Martha anyway."

Without attracting the attention of Martha Frank, George Miller saddled a pony and tied it at the rear of the ranch house. Nancy then slipped out the back door and stole away undetected.

Knowing that she might not have long to work, Nancy made the trip in record time. She tied the pony to a tree and then cautiously approached the cottage. The door was closed, and, after a moment's hesitation, she opened it.

"It's safe enough," she decided after listening. "There's no one here."

Boldly she entered the cottage and went into the bedroom. It required but an instant to drag out the trunk from a closet. The lid was tightly closed, but to her relief she found the trunk unlocked.

Hurriedly, she began to examine the contents. To the dresses and the doll she gave only a passing glance, but a box of jewelry she caught up eagerly. Selecting a locket, she opened it. To her disappointment it did not contain a picture.

"It's been removed," she told herself.

A tiny ring next attracted her attention. Snatching it up, she saw two initials engraved on the inside. The letters were: "L. B."

"Louise Bowen!" Nancy murmured. "Now I am convinced that Lucy and Louise are the same!"

After a moment's thought, she tied the ring in her handkerchief and slipped it into her pocket.

The trunk contained but one more box, and a hasty examination assured Nancy that it was practically empty.

"I have the evidence I need anyway," she decided.

Closing the lid, she pushed the trunk back into place. A strange feeling of uneasiness which she could not understand made her wheel about suddenly. What she saw caused her to start back in consternation.

In the doorway, regarding her with an evil smile, stood Zany Shaw.

CHAPTER XXIII

TRAPPED

A LITTLE cry of surprise and fright escaped Nancy Drew as she saw Zany Shaw regarding her with narrowed eyes. Whether or not he had seen her take the ring she did not know, but there could be no question that he knew what she was about. It angered her that this man had come to interfere with her plans.

"Caught this time!" Zany croaked triumphantly as he moved toward her.

"I'm doing nothing wrong," Nancy defended.

Zany laughed harshly and reaching out caught her wrist in a cruel grip. He raised his arm to strike her.

"I'll teach you to meddle in affairs that don't concern you," he snarled.

Nancy, angered at the threat, wriggled from his grasp. She tried to make a dash for the door, but Zany blocked her path.

"Let me out!"

"Not much I won't!"

The man made another clutch for her arm,

but Nancy dodged quickly enough to elude his grasp. Now thoroughly frightened, she saw that Zany really intended to harm her. As he made a second spring, she struck out with all her might. It was no futile blow. Her fist landed squarely under Zany's chin. He staggered back, clutched at a chair and sagged to the floor.

In mingled horror and triumph, Nancy beheld her handiwork. She saw at a glance that the man was not harmed; he was only stunned. In a few minutes he would have fully recovered from the blow, but before that time it behooved her to be safely away.

Quick as a flash, she darted out of the cottage, sprang on her pony, and rode rapidly toward Shadow Ranch. From a knoll, only a short distance from the ranch, she caught sight of a roadster speeding toward her.

"It must be Doctor Cole coming to see Lucy," she told herself.

In a minute or two the automobile drew near and she saw that she had not been mistaken. Doctor Cole was driving, but to Nancy's surprise he had another man with him. It was not until the doctor stopped the car to greet her that she saw the face of the stranger. It was Ross Rogers.

"Hello," Doctor Cole called pleasantly. "Out early, I see. How is our patient this morning?"

"She was resting comfortably when I left. I've had quite an exciting morning of it myself."

Doctor Cole glanced at her quizzically, but did not question her, taking it for granted that she did not wish to talk before a stranger.

"Pardon us," he said, "I didn't think to ask. Of course you've met Ross Rogers?"

"Oh, yes, indeed."

"I thought he was looking as though he needed fresh air, so I brought him along for the ride."

Nancy bestowed a friendly smile upon Mr. Rogers, yet she could not but remember the strange way he had left Shadow Ranch at his last call. Undoubtedly, Doctor Cole had not told him where he was going when they had set out. Otherwise, she doubted that he would have made the trip, for though he was friendly enough upon occasions, he seemed to be afraid that Nancy and her friends would subject him to embarrassing questions.

After making a few more inquiries concerning his patient, Doctor Cole drove slowly on toward Shadow Ranch. Nancy urged her pony into a gallop and arrived only a few minutes behind. In fact, as she swung into the yard, she saw Doctor Cole getting his leather bag from the rear end of the roadster.

He waited until Nancy had tied her pony to

the fence and then walked toward the house
with her. Nancy was eager to tell her friend
what she had discovered at the cottage, but as
Ross Rogers was following only a few steps
behind, decided that it would be wiser to wait.
Nevertheless, as she walked up the path, she
cast a quick glance around to see if Martha
were still on the premises.

"I mean to have a talk with her," she
thought.

Martha had squatted on the steps of the
veranda and as Nancy and the doctor approached she reluctantly arose to make way
for them to pass. She cast a glance of undisguised hatred at the two, and then her eyes
focused upon Ross Rogers. An instant she
stared at the man in blank amazement and the
color left her face. Throwing up her hands
as though to ward off a blow, she began to
gibber.

As Nancy stared at the woman in surprise,
she gave a little scream and ran toward the
gate.

"Stop her!" Nancy shouted. "Don't let her
get away!"

Martha reached the gate, but there her
escape was cut off by George Miller who
was coming to the house with a milk pail on
his arm.

"Hold on!" he said gruffly, catching the

woman firmly by the arm. "What's your hurry there, Martha?"

"Let me go! Let me go!" Martha screamed, struggling wildly to free herself.

By this time the commotion had brought Mrs. Rawley and the girls out of the ranch house.

"What is going on out here?" Mrs. Rawley demanded somewhat sternly. "Lucy is asleep."

"I don't know what it's all about, ma'am," George told her, feeling that he was about to be censured. "Miss Nancy yelled out for me to stop her, so that's what I did. Oh, no, you don't!" This as Martha renewed her attempt to escape.

"I believe I must have frightened the woman," Ross Rogers declared. "She looked at me and then began to mumble things I couldn't understand."

"Is there any need to hold her?" Mrs. Rawley asked, turning to Nancy. "If she is willing to leave——"

"Yes, I have an excellent reason for stopping her," Nancy announced. "I want to ask her where she got this?"

She drew her handkerchief from her pocket and unwrapped the ring which she had found in the trunk. At the sight of the jewelry, Martha made a last frantic effort to free herself.

Her efforts were futile. The foreman held her in an ironlike grip.

"Where did you get this?" Nancy repeated, when the woman had quieted down.

Martha shrugged her shoulders, but not a word did she answer.

"So you've lost your tongue?" Nancy demanded. "You can talk all right when it's to your advantage."

Martha regarded her sullenly.

"Will you answer my question willingly, or must I find a way to force you?"

Again the woman shrugged her shoulders. Nancy was becoming exasperated, but remembering that Martha's attempt to escape apparently had been occasioned by the sight of Ross Rogers, she turned to the man hopefully.

"Do you know anything about this woman?" she questioned.

Mr. Rogers shook his head.

"Nothing except hearsay. I never set eyes on her until to-day. I have no idea what made her act the way she did."

As the man delivered himself of this, Martha eyed him first in fear and then in utter astonishment. The expression was not lost upon Nancy.

"You can't hold me," Martha declared boldly. "I've done nothing wrong."

"That remains to be seen," Nancy told her sternly.

For a moment she stood lost in thought. What could she do to make the woman tell what she knew? Unquestionably, she was more sure of herself since Ross Rogers had said that he did not know her. Suddenly an idea came to Nancy. Turning to Bess, she commanded tersely:

"Get David Glaston on the telephone and tell him to come out here just as quickly as he can. If I can't make her talk, we'll see what a lawyer can do!"

CHAPTER XXIV

Martha Unburdens Herself

"A lawyer!" Martha Frank gasped, her eyes dilating with fear.

"Yes, I intend to send for him unless you tell me everything," Nancy declared.

"I don't know a thing about Lucy. I——"

"Ah, that means you do know a great deal, for I've not mentioned her name!" Nancy caught her up triumphantly. She turned to Bess, who had paused in the doorway. "Go on, Bess. Call Mr. Glaston."

Bess vanished into the ranch house, reappearing in five minutes to announce that the lawyer would drive at once to Shadow Ranch. While they were waiting for his arrival, Nancy tried several times without success to force Martha to tell her story. The woman became sullen and refused to say a word.

At last, to the relief of all concerned, the lawyer's automobile was sighted down the road, and he soon drove into the yard. Nancy lost no time in telling him how matters stood.

He put several questions to Martha but it was not until she was threatened with the authorities that she agreed to talk. So cleverly did the lawyer examine her that she soon contradicted herself and was in a hopeless tangle of falsehoods. It was apparent to all present that she was guilty, and yet the truth could not be forced from her.

Nancy determined upon a bold stroke. Eyeing the woman sharply, she said:

"It doesn't matter what you say. We all know that you kidnapped Lucy from a family in Philadelphia. I have proof——"

There was no need for her to continue. Martha had begun a vehement denial.

"I didn't! I didn't! It was—" she broke off, suddenly aware that she was giving something away.

"Who was it?" the lawyer demanded.

"Zany Shaw," Nancy supplied, watching the woman intently.

Martha sagged back and the defiance melted from her. All at once she looked tired and beaten. She lowered her head and her body shook as though from the ague.

"Wasn't it Zany?" Nancy persisted.

Martha nodded her head listlessly.

"Yes, I'll tell you the entire story, but I want to tell it in my own way."

"Go ahead," the lawyer commanded.

"Zany Shaw is my brother."

"Your brother?" Nancy interrupted involuntarily. "That explains why I saw him so often at your cottage."

"Partially. Eight years ago Zany and I lived in Philadelphia. He had a good job there and we were saving money and paying for a little house of our own."

"Wait a minute," the lawyer broke in. "You say Zany is your brother, but your names aren't the same."

"Zany's real name is Zeke Work. My name was the same before I married. My husband died fifteen years ago."

"I see. Go on with your story."

"Well, we lived comfortably in Philadelphia. Zany worked for a wealthy man by the name of Bowen. He tended the yard and furnace and did odd jobs around the house. Everything went along fine until one day Zany's employer lost some money. It wasn't so much, only fifty dollars. Mr. Bowen asked that all the help be searched, and as luck would have it, they found money on Zany."

"You mean he had stolen it?" Nancy questioned.

"No, Zany may have his faults, but he ain't one to steal. The money was his own. We'd been saving it up for several months a little at a time."

"How did he happen to have it in his pocket?" Nancy asked.

"He aimed to make a payment on our house. When Mr. Bowen saw the money he claimed it was his."

"Didn't your brother explain?"

"Yes, but Mr. Bowen wouldn't believe the story. He discharged Zany on the spot and told him he was getting off easy not to be turned over to the police."

"That does seem unjust," Nancy admitted.

"Zany was furious and I didn't blame him. Mr. Bowen wouldn't give him a reference and he couldn't get work. We lost our house and we lost everything. Then Zany made up his mind to get even. I tried to talk him out of it, but he wouldn't listen to me.

"He watched his chance and one night he slipped into the house, took the child from the nursery, gagged her so she couldn't let out a scream, and then sneaked off with her and some of her things."

Nancy nodded. So far Martha's story followed her own theory perfectly and she felt certain that the woman was telling the truth.

"Then what happened?" she prompted.

"Zany managed to get her to the place where we were then living—it was in the poor district of Philadelphia. I opened the door to let him in but just then the child let out a howl. Zany had taken off her gag as soon as he was away from the Bowen's and he didn't think a youngster of three and a half would make any disturbance.''

''Someone heard her screams?'' Nancy prompted.

Martha's eyes wandered to Ross Rogers, who had been an interested listener to the strange story.

''Yes, a man was standing at the curb and he tried to interfere. Zany tried to get away, but this man threatened to call the police. In desperation Zany picked up a piece of iron and threw it at him.

''He was struck squarely on the head and he fell without a word. We dragged him into the house, but we couldn't bring him to. He was as white as a ghost and his heart didn't seem to beat. We worked over him for fifteen minutes and finally gave up. Zany thought he had killed him.

''We were frantic. We didn't know what to do, but we did know we had to get away from Philadelphia. Zany hadn't intended to take the child away from the city, but just hold her for ransom until Mr. Bowen came over handsomely. He had to change his plans.''

''You came West?'' the lawyer inquired.

''Yes, we packed up a few things and got out that same night. We went from one place to

another and finally drifted here. We didn't
go around together for fear people would become suspicious. Zany went into the junk business and made enough to keep us both."

"Did you know that a large reward was offered for the return of the child?" Nancy asked.

"Yes, we saw it in the papers. But we
couldn't take advantage of it. We were afraid
that if we sent Lucy back she'd tell all she knew
and then we'd be accused of murder. We
changed her name from Louise to Lucy and
brought her up to think she didn't have any
mother or father."

"How did you happen to keep that doll and
the little garments Louise was dressed in when
she came to you?" Nancy thought to inquire.
"Weren't you afraid they would sometime give
you away."

"Zany told me I must get rid of them, but I
never did it. The little dresses were so pretty
I couldn't bear to burn them up."

"There's one thing you've forgotten. Who
was the man that Zany accidently killed?"

Again Martha's eyes wandered to Ross
Rogers."

"That's him!" she declared.

"What!" Nancy cried, and her exclamation
of surprise was echoed by the others.

"Zany must not have killed him after all."

"I'm very much alive," Mr. Rogers an-

nounced with a smile. "And, really, this is all
news to me, but I think it explains something
that has troubled me for a great many years."

All eyes were now turned upon the man.

"I owe you all an apology for my recent be-
havior," he began. "I didn't mean to be rude.
I was only troubled by not having a past."

"I'm sure you were never rude," Mrs. Rawley assured him graciously. "But tell us what
you mean by not having a past."

"I will begin where Martha left off," Mr.
Rogers said quietly. "My story may seem dis-
jointed at first, but perhaps you can piece
something out of it. At least I hope you can.

"Eight years ago, I found myself in an old
house which was located in a section of Philadelphia such as Martha Frank has just described. My head throbbed painfully and I felt
as though I had been sick for many days. I
could not remember what had happened to me.
My first thought was that I had been robbed by
a thug, but to my surprise I found several
thousand dollars in bills still in an inside
pocket.

"I was at a loss to know where this money
came from. Possibly I was accustomed to
carry large amounts. Possibly I had just taken
it in payment for a debt. I believe I must have
gone to Philadelphia on a business trip and
through curiosity had ventured into the poor

section. Of course, at the time I remembered none of this, and even now I am not sure as to the truth of it all.

"When I first regained consciousness I was surprised that I could not remember my own name. In fact, I was not certain how much money I had in my possession, for as I have later learned, I suffered from alexia."

"Alexia?" Bess demanded. "What is that?"

"Inability to understand the written word," Doctor Cole explained. "In rare cases it accompanies loss of identity—undoubtedly brought on by severe shock."

"You can imagine my state," Mr. Rogers went on. "I couldn't read and all my efforts to find out who I was failed. Gradually I improved, and the ability to read again came back to me. At last I drifted West and settled in Mougarstown. I opened a little shop, and with the exception of a number of Eastern trips, have remained in the West for the past few years."

"You regained your identity?" George Fayne asked gently.

"Unfortunately, no. I can remember everything that has happened to me since that day eight years ago, but nothing that occurred before. I groped for my name but could never think of it. I finally decided upon Ross Roger, though I know it isn't my real one. Then others changed it to Rogers. It was all the same to me. Now that Martha Frank has told her story, I think it probable that it was I who tried to interfere.''

"You're the man,'' Martha identified him positively. "I'd know you anywhere.''

"But I have met your brother several times on the street. If he recognized me, why wasn't he afraid to remain here?''

"Zany probably didn't have a clear recollection of you. He was so excited that night he didn't know what he was about, poor man.''

"I see. Perhaps now you can tell me who I am.''

Martha shook her head.

"I never set eyes on you before that night.''

"Then it looks as though the mystery of my past isn't to be solved after all,'' Mr. Rogers said sadly. "I had hoped——''

"Just a minute!'' Nancy broke in eagerly. "You say you selected the name Roger. Did you have any particular reason for adopting that name?''

"Why, no. It sounded familiar, and I thought it might possibly be mine.''

"Do you realize what it spells backwards?'' Nancy asked, with growing excitement.

"Regor!'' several in the group announced together after a moment's thought.

"Regor!" the man repeated thoughtfully. "Regor! That does sound strangely familiar. But isn't that the name of the young lady——"

"Yes," Nancy said, gazing at him intently.

Alice's face had gone white and her usual composure had left her. As Ross Rogers turned toward her, she nervously twisted her handkerchief.

"Oh, it couldn't be—" she whispered brokenly.

The man continued to stare at her, searching every line of her face.

"Alice!" he murmured, and stretched out his arms. "Alice!"

CHAPTER XXV

A Happy Ending

As Ross Rogers took a step toward Alice Regor, those who had witnessed the little drama exchanged startled glances. Was it possible that Alice had found her father at last? George Fayne, the first to recover from her surprise, whispered to Nancy:

"They do resemble each other, but it doesn't seem possible they could be related. It would be too dramatic!"

Mr. Rogers had extended his arms to Alice, but as quickly they dropped to his sides again.

"I mustn't jump at conclusions," he said sadly. "For a moment I thought I remembered." He gave an uncertain laugh. "I believed that Alice was really my daughter. Of course, I am mistaken."

"Perhaps not," Nancy observed quietly, turning to Alice, who was still staring at Mr. Rogers with anxious, wistful eyes. "Tell me, do you remember your father?"

"I'm afraid not. He—he disappeared when I was too young. I have only a faint recollection of him, if any at all."

"What was his full name?"

"Robert Ross Regor."

"Ross?" Nancy demanded eagerly. "And in selecting his own name, Mr. Rogers chose Ross. That appears more than mere coincidence to me."

"My husband knew Alice's father well. He was his brother-in-law, you know," Mrs. Rawley put in. "Unfortunately, I never met him myself nor saw his picture."

"If only he were here now!" Nancy cried.

"I could send for him. I am certain that for anything as important as this, he would make the trip. Especially as it concerns Alice's happiness and that of Mrs. Regor."

"If you could telegraph him it would settle everything! Perhaps if he can't come, he can at least send a picture."

"I shall do it at once."

Mrs. Rawley hastened into the ranch house to telephone the Mougarstown telegraph station.

"How about notifying your mother?" Nancy asked Alice.

"Oh, not until we are certain! If it doesn't turn out the way we hope, she would be completely unnerved."

"Of course we'll wait," Nancy agreed. "I didn't think."

"And now what's to be done with Martha Frank and that brother of hers?" George Miller broke in.

"I think that is up to Mr. Rogers," Nancy declared. "As far as I am personally concerned I have no charges to make against either of them, and Lucy's parents are both dead. I feel that they have been punished sufficiently already."

"I agree with you," Mr. Rogers said quietly. "I will not prosecute if they will promise to leave the country at once."

As soon as Martha had agreed to the terms, she was given her freedom and vanished in the direction of her cottage. It may be added that when a number of cowboys from Shadow Ranch visited the cabin a few days later, they found it deserted. Martha, together with Zany Shaw, had fled, in their haste leaving all household furniture behind. They were never heard of again.

"What a wonderful thing for Lucy!" Nancy declared, after Martha was out of sight. "To think that she is really Louise Bowen. With the fortune which has been left in her name, she'll be able to have all the things she needs— clothes, an education, and good times."

"And all due to your clever work," Alice

said earnestly. "Oh, Nancy, I think you're wonderful! And if you really prove that Ross Rogers is my father, I'll be grateful to my dying day."

"I think things will come out all right," Nancy told her kindly. "We'll hope so at any rate."

At Mrs. Rawley's invitation, Ross Rogers consented to remain at Shadow Ranch for the next few days, and Nancy and the others were delighted to see how quickly he became acquainted with Alice.

"If he doesn't turn out to be her father, it's going to be terribly disappointing to everyone," Bess remarked to Nancy as the two sat on the veranda. "They're so admirably suited —both quiet and retiring."

Nancy did not reply, for at that moment she had caught sight of an automobile driving up the road toward the ranch, and she knew that it could not belong to either David Glaston or Doctor Cole.

"Someone is coming here," she observed, getting to her feet.

"It can't be Mr. Rawley. He couldn't possibly get here this soon."

"But it is!" Nancy cried suddenly. "See, he's waving. Call the others, quick!"

She dashed madly down the path and was the first to greet Mr. Rawley, for it was indeed he.

"How did you get here so soon?" she demanded.

"When I received Nell's telegram I just hopped the first west-bound airplane out of Chicago, and landed at an airport about fifty miles from here. Came the rest of the way by automobile."

Mrs. Rawley came hurrying out of the ranch house to greet her husband. Mr. Rogers and Alice, unaware that a visitor had arrived, came sauntering in from the garden. Mr. Rawley caught sight of the two, and the expression of his face changed.

"Robert!" he cried, rushing forward, his hand extended. "Don't you know me?"

Eagerly, Mr. Rogers accepted the proffered hand.

"Then I am really Robert Ross Regor? I can't believe my good fortune! Alice, did you hear? You're my own daughter!"

Alice had heard, and she moved into her father's arms, albeit a trifle shyly. Nancy and her friends, happy at what they had accomplished, tactfully withdrew.

After that there were many glorious days at Shadow Ranch. Lucy, or Louise Bowen as she was now called, rapidly recovered under the care of Doctor Cole, and was able to be about, though her arm remained in a sling. Nancy and the other girls took her to Mougarstown, purchasing a wardrobe which produced a remarkable transformation in the child.

"There's only one thing that troubles me," Nancy remarked one day to Mr. Regor, "and that is, what will be done with Louise. Of course she has a substantial fortune, but I wish I were as certain that she would have a happy home."

"Is that all that troubles you?" Mr. Regor smiled. "That problem is easily solved. Alice and I have taken a decided fancy to Louise and if there is no objection to the plan, we will take her home to Baltimore with us."

"Oh, what a wonderful plan! I can't think of anything nicer for Louise."

All too soon, Mrs. Rawley announced that she and her husband must return to Chicago. Alice and Mr. Regor were eager to leave the West, for the latter had sold his store in Mougarstown and planned to go East to make his future home with Mrs. Regor in Baltimore. Nancy, Bess, and George were not as willing to say good-bye to Shadow Ranch, for they wished that their vacation might stretch on indefinitely.

"Oh, well, we'll come back again," Bess declared. "Uncle Dick and Aunt Nell haven't sold the ranch, and I heard them say to-day that they had taken such a fancy to it they thought they would keep it for themselves."

At last the hour of departure arrived and

after good-byes were regretfully said, George
Miller drove the party to the railroad station.
The train rumbled in, and the girls were bun-
dled into their Pullman. George Fayne was
the last to swing up the steps into the car.
Turning, she looked back at the foreman and
grinned.

"Good-bye," she called.

Mr. Miller opened his lips, but the words did
not come. He swallowed and tried again. The
train began to pull out of the station. Then he
found his voice.

"Good-bye," he called gruffly. "Good-bye—
George."

George nearly collapsed as she sank into the
seat beside her friends.

"Did you hear that?" she demanded. "He
actually called me George—and he swore he
wouldn't! I guess I won after all!"

The long trip to Chicago was somewhat tiring, but everyone enjoyed it immensely.

True to his promise, Mr. Regor had taken
Louise Bowen East with him, arrangements
having been made by wire with the Philadelphia
Trust Bank that had her fortune in charge.

At last Chicago was reached, and there another joyful scene was enacted, for Mrs. Regor,
unable to wait longer for a glimpse of her husband, had hurried from Baltimore to meet the
party en route. She, too, was instantly taken

with little Louise Bowen and applauded her husband's decision.

Nancy Drew and her friends had been pleased to observe that a remarkable change had come over Mr. Regor since he had learned his identity. Gradually, he had lost his embarrassed manner which undoubtedly had been caused by the mental turmoil occasioned by his lack of a past. He became almost jovial and George and Bess wondered that they had ever criticised him.

Needless to say, Nancy Drew was highly praised for the good work she had accomplished. Several times Mr. Regor attempted to persuade her to accept a material proof of his gratitude, but at last gave it up as a hopeless task. Nor would Nancy accept the reward which had been offered for information concerning Louise Bowen.

After spending several days in Chicago, Nancy said good-bye to her friends and took the night train for River Heights. As she had hoped, her father met her at the station.

"Glad to see you back," he told her. "It's been mighty lonesome at the old homestead since you left."

Long before they reached the Drew residence, he had learned the details of her exciting summer at Shadow Ranch.

"Two mysteries at one clip!" Carson Drew

whistled softly. "You discovered Louise Bowen and you found Alice Regor's father. I call that clever work, especially for a quiet summer."

"It didn't turn out to be as quiet as I expected," Nancy admitted, with a laugh. "In fact, it was about the most exciting summer I ever had in my life."

"If you keep on the way you've started, you'll surely edge your old dad out of his practice yet."

Nancy gave her father's arm an affectionate pinch.

"You don't seem a bit worried! I guess you know that I couldn't have solved the mystery if you hadn't looked into those Philadelphia files for me."

"You did the thinking. I'm beginning to think it may be wise to protect my practice by taking you in as a partner."

Nancy smiled, highly flattered at the praise her father had bestowed upon her.

"All right," she declared eagerly. "Put out your sign. 'Carson Drew and Daughter.'"

THE END

This Isn't All!

Look on the following pages and you will find listed a few of the outstanding boys' and girls' books published by Grosset and Dunlap. All are written by well known authors and cover a wide variety of subjects—aviation, stories of sport and adventure, tales of humor and mystery—books for every mood and every taste and every pocketbook.